Sport

Editor: Danielle Lobban

Volume 411

independence
educational publishers

First published by Independence Educational Publishers

The Studio, High Green

Great Shelford

Cambridge CB22 5EG

England

ISBN-13: 978 1 86168 870 5

Printed in Great Britain

Zenith Print Group

Contents

Introduction

SPORT is Volume 411 in the **issues** series. The aim of the series is to offer current, diverse information about important issues in our world, from a UK perspective.

ABOUT SPORT

Sport is an important part of many people's social and cultural lives, whether they are participants or spectators. It can enhance health and wellbeing, it brings individuals and communities together and promotes fairness, teamwork, inclusion and respect. This book explores both the beneficial and problematic aspects surrounding sport today, including accessibility, sexism, inequality and profiteering among other issues.

OUR SOURCES

Titles in the **issues** series are designed to function as educational resource books, providing a balanced overview of a specific subject.

The information in our books is comprised of facts, articles and opinions from many different sources, including:

♦ Newspaper reports and opinion pieces

♦ Website factsheets

♦ Magazine and journal articles

♦ Statistics and surveys

♦ Government reports

♦ Literature from special interest groups.

A NOTE ON CRITICAL EVALUATION

Because the information reprinted here is from a number of different sources, readers should bear in mind the origin of the text and whether the source is likely to have a particular bias when presenting information (or when conducting their research). It is hoped that, as you read about the many aspects of the issues explored in this book, you will critically evaluate the information presented.

It is important that you decide whether you are being presented with facts or opinions. Does the writer give a biased or unbiased report? If an opinion is being expressed, do you agree with the writer? Is there potential bias to the 'facts' or statistics behind an article?

ASSIGNMENTS

In the back of this book, you will find a selection of assignments designed to help you engage with the articles you have been reading and to explore your own opinions. Some tasks will take longer than others and there is a mixture of design, writing and research-based activities that you can complete alone or in a group.

FURTHER RESEARCH

At the end of each article we have listed its source and a website that you can visit if you would like to conduct your own research. Please remember to critically evaluate any sources that you consult and consider whether the information you are viewing is accurate and unbiased.

Useful Websites

www.birmingham.ac.uk

www.bylinetimes.com

www.independent.co.uk

www.inews.co.uk

www.ipsos.com

www.metro.co.uk

www.news-decoder.com

www.paralympics.org.uk

www.sportengland.org

www.sporthumanrights.org

www.sportsintegrityinititative.com

www.telegraph.co.uk

www.theconversation.com

www.thecritic.co.uk

England win Euro 2022: how women's football beat the sceptics to breathe new life into the game

An article from The Conversation.

THE CONVERSATION

By John Williams, Senior Lecturer, Department of Sociology, University of Leicester

England's women have won the European football championship, bringing a major international trophy home for the first time since the men's team won the World Cup in 1966, more than a lifetime ago for many of the fans who crowded into Wembley Stadium for the match. They beat Germany, English football's bitterest rival, by two goals to one, in a tense and hard-fought match that was not decided until the second period of extra time.

England's women footballers have not just won the championship, though. The team has captured the public imagination. Attendance at the match was 87,192, the biggest crowd for a Euros football match for either men's or women's football. Newspapers are devoting multiple pages to women's sports coverage and England's key players are becoming well known.

And the games themselves are attracting a whole new set of fans. Watching women's international football feels like – and is – a different world from the men's version. Crowds at men's football are ageing, but at women's football, price, civility and increased safety means that around half the crowd can often be children.

I took my own football-playing ten-year-old granddaughter to see Germany beat France in the semi-final at Stadium MK in Milton Keynes last week. Women and girls outnumbered men and boys comfortably at that game – and booze was of less-than-secondary significance. Inclusivity, participation and diversity were the watchwords here, rather than partisanship and casual abuse of the opposition and its fans.

Infamously, the FA effectively banned women's football in England in 1921 and it took more than 70 years for the governing body to embrace the women's game. But the public profile of UK women's sport has increased considerably. The live TV coverage in Britain of the FIFA Women's World Cup in Canada in 2015 was the first time a UK national broadcaster, the BBC, had covered an international women's sporting event on this scale.

When the women's Euros were last held in the UK in 2005, few people seemed to care. Matches were mainly played in minor venues in the north of England and few were televised. Things have changed, and women's team sport has been thriving on increased media exposure, particularly on free-to-air channels.

Is this a 'sea-change' in the attitudes of the UK government, television companies and the British public to women's sport? Or simply a commercial response to the dearth of live men's sport on non-subscription channels? Or is it, perhaps, a convenient confluence of all?

Overcoming prejudice

Along with colleagues, Stacey Pope and Jamie Cleland, I conducted online research on women and men's reactions to coverage of the women's game soon after the 2015 World Cup finals. Some of this work has only recently been published.

We found that some men – a substantial minority – were highly critical of the extensive TV coverage, arguing that it far outstripped public interest in women's sport. For them, a small 'politically-correct lobby' was ensuring that 'worthless' women's team sport was increasingly widely covered and was now beyond critique on the BBC.

But other men contended that ingrained prejudice remained the key barrier to greater acceptance for women in sport. 'Many football fans remain misogynistic,' affirmed a male Birmingham City fan (36–45), while a Gillingham fan (male, 46–55) was similarly pessimistic, claiming that: "There is still the lingering 'stone age" thinking from some men regarding women in football, which is so entrenched that you will never change them.'

Some of our female respondents were angry at the anti-women sentiments commonly expressed on social media: 'Not just sexism, downright misogyny. Some of the comments I saw on Twitter during the women's World Cup were a disgrace.' (Female, 46–55, Norwich City.) Will this also be part of some men's responses to the current finals? We will need to review the evidence.

Respondents who had attended women's football matches often reflected very positively on the game and its social impact: 'The clubs seem to encourage families and children to attend by having mascots and fun fairs before the game' said a female Wrexham fan (22–25). She went on: 'The atmosphere was great and no need for segregation. It was nice to sit and watch a game of football without bad language too.'

It was also argued that the women's game was different, not inferior, to the men's equivalent: 'I have watched football my whole life and the stereotype [that] women's football is slow and boring is rubbish. Different styles of football occur all over the world; you still want your team to win and it's still exciting.' (Female, 22-25, Bolton Wanderers.)

Better sports?

Top women's football is far better resourced in England today and it is also consciously promoted by the Football Association as a 'cleaner', more wholesome, version of the sport. As one fan (male, 36–45, Liverpool) put it back in 2015: 'One of the main things I have noticed in the woman's game is the lack of diving and the higher level of respect and sportsmanship. This is even evident in the junior football I watch where the girls are lot more respectful to the ref and other players than in the boys' junior game.'

As top women players start to earn higher salaries, perhaps negatives identified above will start to show more in women's football too? I certainly saw signs in Germany v France, for example, of more conscious attempts by women, professionally, to 'game' the referee.

And how will the summer of 2022 affect crowds next season at domestic Women's Super League matches? Problems identified in 2015 were that WSL club venues were small with poor facilities, were difficult to reach and unfamiliar to regular football attenders. All these remain an issue today.

Women's football (and women's sport more generally) is likely to be demanding much more press coverage and air time in the future. It will also perhaps provide new role models for sporting girls – such as my granddaughter – who may begin to see more realistic job prospects in women's team sport. Perhaps football in England is coming home in more ways than one..

29 July 2022

Updated: 31 July 2022

This article has been updated to reflect the outcome of the Euro 2022 final.

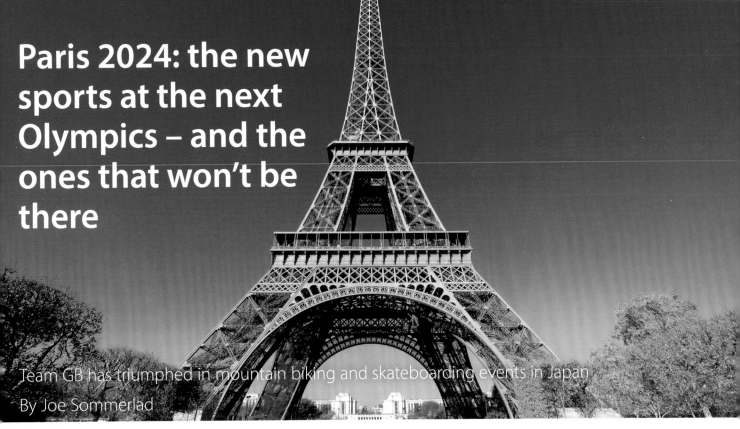

Paris 2024: the new sports at the next Olympics – and the ones that won't be there

Team GB has triumphed in mountain biking and skateboarding events in Japan

By Joe Sommerlad

Despite significant doubts about the wisdom of going ahead with the Tokyo Olympics - even a year on from its initial postponement - with the coronavirus pandemic still raging, the Games have proven a triumph, packed with incident, astonishing personal stories and remarkable achievements.

Spectators gripped by the action in their living rooms across the world have been particularly enthralled by the new sports added to the 2020 roster like skateboarding, mountain biking, sport climbing and surfing.

From the 12 and 13-year-old competitors like Britain's Sky Brown executing gravity-defying tricks and collecting medals at the Ariake Urban Sports Park to the climbers scrambling up artificial walls to slam a buzzer at the summit in less than six seconds, the new additions have kept audiences rapt and ushered in a next generation of household names.

For those already looking ahead to the next instalment of the Summer Games, Paris 2024, the good news is that all four sports will be back next time around and joined by a potentially even more thrilling discipline: break dancing.

Explaining the surprise addition, the head of the Paris organising committee Tony Estanguet said in June 2019 that the emphasis would be on appealing to youth and ensuring the Games were 'more urban' and 'more artistic'.

'The International Olympic Committee (IOC) is keen to set a new standard for inclusive, gender-balanced and youth-centred games,' the Paris Games says on its website.

'Paris 2024 submitted its proposal to the IOC to integrate four new sports that are closely associated with youth and reward creativity and athletic performance. These sports are breaking, sport climbing, skateboarding, surfing. All four are easy to take up and participants form communities that are very active on social media. Over the next five years, the inclusion of these events in the Olympic Games will help inspire millions of children to take up sport.'

Break dancing, or 'breaking', was a hit with the crowds when it was included at the 2018 Youth Olympic Games in Buenos Aires, Argentina, where the men's competition was won by Russia's Sergei Chernyshev (AKA 'Bumblebee') and the women's by Ramu Kawai (AKA 'Ram') of Japan.

Other sports that campaigned for inclusion among the 32 to be showcased in 2024 but which were ultimately unsuccessful were chess, billiards and squash, while baseball and karate will not be returning next time out.

Because of the suspension of the Tokyo Games last summer, the next instalment of the Olympics is now just three years away, taking place in the French capital from 26 July to 11 August 2024.

6 August 2021.

The Olympic games: tarnished but clinging to their ideals

Dogged by corruption and politics, the Olympic Games may seem outmoded. But their ideals survive, and the Games motivate athletes and excite fans.

By Paul Radford

Until COVID-19 uprooted life as we know it, the place of the Olympic Games at the pinnacle of the international sports calendar looked unshakeable.

Yet the postponement of last year's Summer Games in Tokyo and rumblings over their uncertain future have prompted a previously barely whispered question: 'What is the point of the Olympics?'

Burdened by their chequered history and weighed down by puzzling traditions, the Olympic Games' survival into the 21st Century seems a modern miracle when viewed under the spotlight.

If the Olympics did not exist, would there be a clamour to invent them? That's a tough question to answer in the affirmative.

Yet, I suggest it would be unwise to underestimate the validity of the Olympics or their unique values.

The Olympic Games refuse to give up on their ideals

First, full disclosure. I am an unabashed Olympics fan. As a journalist, I covered 17 Summer and Winter Games between 1984 and 2014. I saw first-hand how laudably high-minded sporting ideals can fall foul of drug cheats, corrupt officials and unprincipled coaches.

I have witnessed well-intended attempts by Olympic chiefs to promote peaceful political initiatives come to a grinding halt.

But, like a dogged athlete who turns failures into eventual success, the Olympic movement refuses to give up on its ideals. I think this is what I admire most.

With the exception of the minority who declare no interest in sport, most of us took inspiration when we were young from sporting heroes. I looked to Hungarian soccer captain Ferenc Puskas, Brazilian tennis star Maria Bueno and Australian middle-distance runner Herb Elliott.

But few of us realise that the sporting hero pre-dates the modern mass media by some 2,000 years and is rooted in the Ancient Olympics.

Athletes were feted throughout Greece

Recognised as beginning in Greece in 776 BCE, the Games were at once a test of sporting excellence, a political tool used by city states to assert dominance over rivals, a religious festival and an excuse for a huge party.

Staged at Olympia every four years, the Games endured for more than 1,000 years until they were banned for religious reasons in 394 CE.

Contestants had to be male — and were obliged to prove it by competing naked. There were races, throwing disciplines, combat sports and eventually equestrian events, including chariot racing.

Early sporting heroes included runner Leonidas of Rhodes, who won 12 gold medals, a feat unrivalled until American swimmer Michael Phelps secured his 13th Olympic title in 2016.

Leonidas and other victors such as wrestler Milo of Croton and boxer Theagenes of Thasos were feted for their deeds throughout the Greek world with the same hero worship major athletes receive today.

Elements of amateur days remain

The idea of a modern Olympics was the brainchild of French aristocrat Pierre de Coubertin, an idealist who saw the importance of promoting physical education among the young. He believed athletic competition could promote cross-cultural understanding and peace, and he was convinced there was nobility in the struggle to overcome an opponent.

For de Coubertin, doing one's best was more important than winning.

Through his efforts, the modern Olympics were launched in Athens in 1896. Barring two world wars and now a global pandemic, they have been held every four years since.

De Coubertin's sporting ideals largely persist to this day, although some of his beliefs may look outmoded. He followed the ancients in seeing sport as the preserve of males, and no women participated in the inaugural Games.

He believed in the purity of amateurism. It was not until 1986 that the decision was made to admit professionals to the Games. Even then, individual sports were allowed to bar paid athletes, and some, notably boxing and wrestling, did so for some time.

Still, elements of the amateur days remain. Advertising billboards, commonplace in sports arenas everywhere, are not allowed in Olympic stadiums. Sponsor names are not displayed on team kit, and no prize money is paid by organisers to competitors.

In reality, these ideals are somewhat undermined by the harsh economic reality that a gigantic global event involving more than 10,000 athletes cannot be staged without sponsors. The International Olympic Committee (IOC) raises a large part of its funds from selling marketing rights to a handful of global corporations, such as Coca-Cola, in deals worth hundreds of millions of dollars.

Prize money may not be on offer, but many individual national Olympic Committees pay athletes lucrative bonuses for the medals they win.

A touchy relationship with politics

If the Olympics have a slightly awkward relationship with money, they have an even more delicate one with global politics.

The Games provided a surrogate battleground during the Cold War between the Soviet bloc and Western nations. In the second half of the 20th Century, the Soviet Union and its allies, notably East Germany, poured resources into sport to demonstrate the supposed superiority of the Communist system over the Capitalist West.

Promising athletes were identified at young ages and introduced into a state system of full-time training, while being labelled students, soldiers or state employees to skirt a ban on professionals. There were always widespread suspicions of state-sponsored doping programmes, some of which came to light years later.

The tensions exploded with tit-for-tat boycotts in the 1980s. First, the United States and some other Western nations refused to take part in the 1980 Moscow Summer Games on the grounds that Soviet troops were occupying Afghanistan. In retaliation, the Soviet Union and most of its Eastern European partners boycotted the 1984 Olympics in Los Angeles.

The Olympics were already on their knees after a Palestinian assault on the Israeli team at the 1972 Olympics in Munich had ended in a deadly shootout with German police. Eleven Israeli team members died as well as five of the Black September guerrilla group and one policeman.

Four years later, most African nations refused to take part in the 1976 Montreal Games to protest against a New Zealand rugby tour of then apartheid South Africa.

Some grand gestures flopped

The Olympics might well have gone under. That they did not is often attributed to the calm leadership and diplomatic skill of Spaniard Juan Antonio Samaranch, who took over as IOC president in 1980, introduced reforms and stayed for more than two decades.

Nevertheless, some IOC grand gestures flopped. Seoul was awarded the 1988 Olympics in the hope that this would lead to the reunification of North and South Korea. In the end, despite some frantic diplomatic activity, North Korea declined to participate, and the opportunity disappeared.

Twenty years later, for similar reasons, the 2008 Games went to Beijing in the hope that this would lead to the

opening up of China to the world and increased respect for human rights within its borders.

It all went wrong early on when China's pledge to allow free internet access turned out to be not what it seemed. Internet access within the Olympics was not matched elsewhere in the country, with restrictions retained among the population in general.

The IOC itself has hardly been beyond reproach.

In 1998, a whistle-blower revealed that members of the IOC had taken bribes or received gifts from officials of the Salt Lake City Olympic bid team for the 2002 Winter Games. The affair lifted the lid on an ongoing scandal around Olympic bids. Ten IOC members were expelled, 10 more sanctioned and reforms were made to ensure no repeat.

There have been great successes

But it would be wrong to dwell on failures when there have been great successes. Progressive strides have been made on gender equality towards the ideal of a 50-50 split between male and female competitors. At the 2016 Olympics in Rio de Janeiro, there were more than 5,000 female athletes, some 47% of the total.

The Olympic movement has been a world leader in disabled sport. The Paralympic Games, which started in 1960, have become a huge global event, with more than 4,000 athletes participating in the last Summer event in Rio.

My personal conversion to the Olympics started with a reporting assignment to the Olympic village in Sarajevo in 1984. Seeing the excitement of hundreds of Olympic athletes from all over the world eating together in a mass canteen, playing ping pong and exchanging experiences despite language barriers was eye-opening.

There are exceptions, but to this day most Olympic athletes prefer living in a village with thousands of international competitors rather than being isolated in a five-star hotel. It is hard to imagine a better way to promote international friendship among young people.

The unique atmosphere of an Olympics permeates host cities. I never imagined that the vibrant ambience I had witnessed in Barcelona, Sydney or Vancouver would prevail when in 2012 the Olympics came to my then home city of London.

But Britons' natural reserve evaporated as Londoners celebrated with almost wild abandon, showing generous hospitality to international visitors that was not always evident in the past.

It is probably only the Olympic Games that could achieve that.

15 June 2021

Former global sports editor at Reuters, Paul Radford has covered 17 Olympic Games, seven World Cups and numerous world championships in more than 20 sports. He was sports editor for 12 years at the end of a career that included assignments in Germany and Paris. Formerly a consultant to the International Olympic Committee, he served on the IOC's press commission for 15 years and was editor-in-chief of the official Olympic News service at the 2014 Winter Olympics in Sochi, Russia.

Three questions to consider:

1. Can the Olympics justify its leading place on the world stage or has it become too costly, unwieldy and environmentally unfriendly?

2. Should the Games be awarded only to countries with a strong human rights record?

3. Should athletes found guilty of doping or other forms of cheating be barred for life, or should they be allowed to take part in the Games after they have completed a term of suspension?

ParalympicsGB make history at Beijing 2022

An array of outstanding performances ensured ParalympicsGB were more competitive in more sports than ever before at Beijing 2022.

A succession of memorable results saw the British team continue to build on the progress of recent Winter Games, winning six medals including some landmark successes and a host of top five finishes.

Our most competitive squad

The team's youngest athlete, Neil Simpson, 19, guided by his brother Andrew, became the first British man to win a gold medal on snow with victory in the Super G and quickly followed that up with bronze in the Super Combined.

Menna Fitzpatrick, competing at these Games with guide Gary Smith, became the most decorated British Winter Paralympian in history with six medals in total after winning silver in the Super G and bronze in the Super Combined to add to the four she won at PyeongChang 2018.

Millie Knight and Brett Wild won ParalympicsGB's first medal of Beijing 2022, and now have four in total, with bronze in the Downhill on day one of competition.

Ollie Hill secured ParalympicsGB's first ever Para snowboard medal with a bronze in the banked slalom.

> *'These have been an historic games for ParalympicsGB with so many magical performances across the team.'*
>
> –Phil Smith, ParalympicsGB Chef de Mission

'This is the most competitive squad we have ever taken to a Paralympic Winter Games and is testament to all the hard work, excellence and incredible resilience of the athletes and the support staff that I have the privilege to work with and call teammates.

'We couldn't have achieved this success without the support of UK Sport and National Lottery players and I would like to thank them for helping make so many sporting dreams come true to unite and inspire the nation once again.'

Katherine Grainger, Chair of UK Sport, said: 'ParalympicsGB are once again returning with an impressive set of medals and Beijing marks the third successive winter Games that a British athlete has reached the top of the podium. That's a positive sign of developing consistency and helps our wider aim for winter sports to become an ever-greater force in British sport.

'We are thankful for the role of Government and The National Lottery continue to play in providing the financial support that enables athletes to pursue their dreams. Following the excitement and inspiration of these Winter Games we are optimistic for the future for winter sports and are committed to making them ever more relevant and accessible as we now look towards Milan-Cortina in 2026.'

But the medal success tells only half the story of the progress achieved in a range of Winter disciplines. There have been 13 top five finishes (including medals) at Beijing 2022 which is the most ever by a ParalympicsGB team at a Winter Games.

ParalympicsGB had a team of 24 athletes competing at Beijing 2022, the biggest since Lillehammer 1994. There were an incredible 13 Paralympic debuts (David Melrose, Meggan Dawson-Farrell, Gary Smith, Neil Simpson, Andrew Simpson, Shona Brownlee, Dan Sheen, Alex Slegg, Callum Deboys, Hope Gordon, Steve Arnold, Ollie Hill and Andy MacLeod).

James Barnes-Miller and Owen Pick achieved top five finishes in Para snowboard. Hope Gordon became ParalympicsGB's first ever female Nordic skier when she competed in the Women's sprint seated cross country and Scott Meenagh achieved the best result of his Paralympic career finishing in sixth place in the long-distance seated Biathlon.

There was also a highest finish at his third Paralympic Games for James Whitley with sixth in the Giant Slalom, while the Wheelchair Curling team had some notable victories including an 10-6 success against the USA who finished fifth in the competition.

13 March 2022

5 sport and human rights issues to look out for in 2022

Climate action in sport

Sport will be urged to help connect the climate and human rights agendas

Sport can't be a bystander in ongoing climate change debates and responses. Mounting threats of extreme weather, including floods, fires and rising temperatures, will increasingly impact the sporting events calendar and infrastructure, and pose greater risks to the health and wellbeing of athletes and fans, particularly the young and old who are most vulnerable. The year 2022 will likely bring greater scrutiny to how sport at every level is addressing the climate crisis and making connections to responsibilities for respecting and protecting human rights.

There are important examples of sport leaders engaging on the climate agenda. Nearly 300 sports federations and members of the wider sport ecosystem have signed up to the UN's Sport for Climate Action initiative and have committed to reducing their climate impact, as well as advocating for responsible responses. Athlete activists are also highlighting the need for leadership on climate issues.

During 2022, sport leaders will also need to recognise and act on the links between climate change and respect for fundamental human rights. In 2021, the UN Human Rights Council officially recognised the right to a healthy environment and established a new expert mandate on climate change and human rights. What do these developments mean for sport?

Sport leaders have an opportunity to take targeted steps to scale up their own human rights due diligence in ways that account for actual and potential adverse impacts on people connected to climate change. This may cover a wide range of issues, from harms to individuals and communities relating to loss and damage of sport infrastructure, to land development decisions and use of scarce water supplies, to

safety concerns for athletes relating to extreme heat, among many others.

The world of sport should also contribute to wider initiatives addressing the rights of those most vulnerable to climate change. Given that global sport has a significant emissions footprint globally, it is time for all involved to engage in constructive steps to manage the many transitions that are needed to address the climate crisis for those impacted today and for future sport loving generations to come.

Cementing human rights in sports governance

Calls will expand for leaders to fully integrate human rights in sport governance and culture

Many human rights challenges facing the sport sector can be traced back to issues of governance, leadership and culture. Sports integrity and safe sport initiatives are certainly part of the solution, but human rights are much broader and integrating these concerns into the fabric of sport requires people-centric measures to address current and historical power imbalances and protect vulnerable stakeholders.

In 2022, expectations of those in leadership positions across sport will likely intensify with calls to set the tone on human rights risks and responses. That will require leading by example, and ensuring good governance and fair processes at all levels of sport. This is necessary to make governance structures fit for purpose in human rights terms.

In sport, responsible leadership is especially important. The sector is characterised by a high degree of autonomy and self-regulation on the basis that sport is much more than a commercial proposition. Indeed, the Revised European Sports Charter sets out that sport should enjoy autonomous decision-making processes and choose its leaders democratically, with governments and sports organisations recognising the need for mutual respect. In this context, if sport is truly to serve society, then autonomy should be underpinned by a strong social licence and clear systems of accountability. Those in leadership positions will need to continue to demonstrate a proactive willingness to participate in meaningful stakeholder engagement with those impacted by their decisions and to strengthen their individual and collective commitments towards the prevention and mitigation of harm. This includes sports bodies making daily efforts to gain and maintain the trust of athletes, local communities and all others they seek to represent and serve through their activities.

Tackling systemic issues including discrimination and sexual abuse now requires bold, empathetic and respectful leadership together with sincere levels of humility, transparency and openness within sports governance in order to create cultures that are truly fair, accessible, inclusive, and enabling. This means acknowledging, managing and mitigating conflicts of interest. It also means transforming structures and systems to ensure greater diversity and representation within governance and management frameworks, including, in searches for talent to run sports bodies, as well as the adoption of robust codes of conduct that can be relied upon. Good governance also must include independent and transparent investigations and effective remedy processes when things go wrong.

The year ahead will see continued efforts by a range of actors to develop practical tools, guidance and materials to support sports leaders in the work they must do to adopt human rights commitments, undertake due diligence, and implement robust policy, evaluation and measurement frameworks. For those willing to step up, the roadmaps and support increasingly exist to make a positive difference and strengthen the entire sports ecosystem.

Gender fairness and inclusion

Conversations on fairness and inclusion will increasingly include human rights-based approaches

The rights of transgender athletes and athletes with variations in sex characteristics will continue to be a trending sport and human rights topic in 2022. The conversation is set to move from a focus on the right to participate in competitive sport, towards how inclusion can be managed in ways that respect human rights and ensure safe and fair competition for all. Although it has been argued by some sport entities that fairness and inclusion are two irreconcilable aims under our current sport models, the challenge this year will be to move beyond these opposing views and seek innovative solutions that are, first and foremost, based on respecting the human rights of all athletes participating or competing.

The recently released IOC Framework on Fairness, Inclusion, and non-Discrimination on the basis of Gender Identity and Sex Variations provides initial guidance in that direction, which will evolve. From March 2022 onwards, International Federations (IFs) will be responsible for defining how this framework will work in practice applied to specific sports, disciplines, and events.

The IOC has committed to providing educational webinars and workshops, and more specific guidance for those who request it, in order to support IFs in reassessing and redesigning their policies and eligibility criteria in alignment with the framework's principles. Awareness raising and capacity building for national federations, coaches, and members of athletes' own teams will be key in avoiding misinterpretations and inappropriate use of the rules at the local level. The absence of such steps have caused harm to athletes and must not be repeated. Sports governance at all levels will need to ensure that human rights due diligence processes are undertaken and if unexpected harms do occur, accessible and effective remedy is provided.

2022 will also likely see a significant increase in research conducted in this emerging area, as one of the key recommendations of the IOC framework is that diverse gender identities and variations in sex characteristics should not be assumed as an unquestionable

sign of disproportionate advantage nor imply unavoidable risk to other athletes. Rather, any eligibility rules should be based on ethical, credible, and peer-reviewed research. Keeping human rights approaches at the centre of these developments will be critical in ensuring positive outcomes for all involved.

Overcoming institutional exclusion

Efforts to tackle institutional racism, social injustice and legacies of colonialism in sport will continue to garner global attention

Racism, social injustice and legacies of colonialism in sport are not new, but public demands to take more effective action to address them are set to take on new urgency in 2022 and beyond.

During 2021, a number of events across every continent highlighted the prevalence and harm of racism and discrimination in sport, both on and off the field of play. Examples included relentless racial abuse targeting athletes at various competitions and online; investigations into institutional racism and exclusionary practices in sport teams and clubs; ongoing criticism and debate of athlete advocacy and activism related to social justice issues and continuous scrutiny of sport bodies related to diversity of experiences and representation in leadership roles and structures.

Despite these and other concerning developments globally, there have also been pockets of recent progress that are noteworthy. Governments and public funding bodies are becoming more engaged in providing regulatory support and more explicit guidance in addressing racism and exclusion in sport. Some sport bodies and major event organisers have made formal commitments to enable greater acknowledgement of and representation from people from historically marginalised groups, for example indigenous peoples, persons with disabilities, and women and girls. Broad debates and discussions have developed across a number of sports on universal, accessible and inclusive organisational design and representation in leadership, including from the global south and small, and island, states. There has also been growth in new commercial deals that will provide enhanced global coverage of events from traditionally underrepresented regions.

In reality, such progress is still sporadic and limited, and much more needs to be done. The challenges of lack of representation and equal access are endemic for a variety of social reasons, cultural norms, patriarchal constructs and the legacies of historical injustices and colonialism. In 2022, the sports ecosystem will see renewed calls and campaigns to bolster existing initiatives to transparently address these issues and for new strategies that take a zero tolerance approach to racism and social injustice. If sport and its corporate and broadcast partners can fulfil their responsibilities, be proactive about their duty of care, and be more inclusive, accessible and welcoming, then the foundations can be laid for transformational leadership with real impact for people and communities.

Mental health and health Inequality

Addressing ongoing health impacts of Covid-19 and fresh health issues will be a priority for the sport community

Covid-19 continues to surge in many countries, and is of particular concern in areas with low vaccination rates. The effects of the pandemic on women's sport, public access to sport and the mostly still unknown long-term implications of Covid-19 we raised in 2021 continue to be of concern. Going into 2022, mental health and global health inequalities join this watch list.

The pandemic has brought mental health issues to the fore. The Tokyo Olympics saw high profile athletes pull out of events citing mental health concerns. Since 2020 athlete unions have pushed for athletes, like other workers, to be protected under ILO standards, and for recognition of the importance of mental health. With many of the world's largest sporting events convening this year, 2022 is likely to see more athletes speak up and lobby for their mental health, opening the door for workers, volunteers and others to do the same. Pressure will increase on sport federations, sponsors and others in sport to take seriously and address the mental health of athletes.

Global health inequalities drawn into sharp focus by the pandemic will also be a priority in 2022, including addressing their impacts on global sport events and athletes. The Africa Cup of Nations has been impacted by serious outbreaks of Covid-19 depleting teams' starting line-ups. This led the hosting government of Cameroon to increase testing in a bid to encourage more fans to attend matches. Access to vaccines in the Global South will remain a challenge that needs to be met with urgency and investment this year.

For the upcoming Beijing Winter Olympics, whilst vaccination will not be mandatory for athletes, those not vaccinated will face a full 21 days in quarantine – significantly affecting their preparations for the event, and will disproportionately affect athletes from countries with low vaccination rates, many of them in the Global South. While athletes were prioritised for vaccination ahead of the Tokyo 2020 Olympic Games, it is unclear whether this will be true for the Beijing, or whether this is warranted given the urgency of prioritising at-risk individuals.

The Australian Open controversy over Novak Djokovic and his deportation from Australia raises questions over whether athletes should be offered exemptions to travel when much of the world continues to face quarantines and other constraints, and are a reminder of the ongoing challenge of coordinating rules around events with host government regulations. Vaccination requirements and exemptions for sporting events in 2022 highlight wider health inequalities in society and will likely to continue be scrutinised.

2 February 2022

Activity levels see partial recovery from Covid-19

People are returning to sport and physical activity but opportunities remain unequal, latest data finds.

Activity levels are starting to recover following large drops caused by coronavirus (Covid-19) pandemic restrictions, our latest *Active Lives Adult Survey* report shows.

Covering the period between November 2020 and November 2021, the results, which have been published today, show that while activity levels obviously dropped as a result of restrictions designed to stop the spread of the virus, they then stabilised and are now starting to recover.

Between November 2020 and November 2021, 61.4% of the population were active, and 27.2% were inactive. The recovery started in mid-March 2021 when there was a rise of 3% to 61.2% of the population getting active (between mid-March – mid-May), compared to just 58.2% 12 months earlier.

While numbers are still down compared to pre-pandemic, with 600k (1.9%) fewer active adults and 1.3 million (2.6%) more inactive adults, the recovery is a testament to the work and investment that went into helping people stay active during a period of unprecedented restrictions.

However, while this initial recovery is good news, the data shows that this is not universal, with many people struggling, a trend that emerged before the pandemic and which is why our strategy, Uniting the Movement, has such a strong focus on tackling inequalities and barriers.

When restrictions were lifted in July 2021, the number of people saying they felt they had the opportunity to be active increased close to levels we saw pre the emergence of coronavirus.

Team sports participation numbers bounced back close to pre-pandemic levels, following large drops during restrictions. Football (+2% across mid-July – mid-September 2021), cricket (+0.3% mid-July – mid-September 2021) and basketball (+0.3% mid-September – mid-November 2021) in particular have seen large numbers of returners which is driving the overall recovery in team sports.

However, because pre-pandemic, the numbers taking part in team sports were declining, we are continuing to support this part of our sector to recover and to reinvent how it provides opportunities to play sport and get active. This builds on the £270 million of funding we provided to support grassroots sport and physical activity early on during the most severe restrictions and includes our continuing multi-million investment into community sport facilities.

There is positive news for older people with recovery to pre-pandemic levels seen in activity levels for those aged 55-74 and 75+ while the report is also clear which audiences continue to struggle.

We continue to work closely with partners across the sport and physical activity landscape, not just to drive demand and increase participation, but also to ensure the long-term viability of the sector through a focus on work in areas like safeguarding, coaching, governance and leadership development.

Overall population numbers hide stark inequalities with women, those from ethnically diverse communities, those living in more deprived areas, disabled people and people with long-term health conditions still less likely to be active than others, and the pandemic has exacerbated the

Inactive	**Fairly active**	**Active**
Less than an average of 30 minutes a week	An average of 30-49 minutes a week	An average of 150+ minutes a week
27.2%	11.5%	61.4%
27.2% of people (12.4m) did less than an average of 30 minutes a week	11.5% (5.2m) were fairly active but didn't reach an average of 150 minutes a week	61.4% (28.0m) did an average of 150 minutes or more a week

inequalities for the least affluent, Asian people, disabled people and people with long-term health conditions in particular.

The gap in activity levels between the haves and have nots has also widened during the pandemic, with those that live in deprived areas seeing bigger drops in activity levels than those in more well-off areas. For example, activity fell 4.4% for those living in the most deprived areas (IMD 1-3) compared to pre-pandemic compared to a 1.2% for those in the least deprived areas (IMD 8-10).

This is why our strategy, Uniting the Movement, has a strong focus on tackling inequalities and levelling up, and why we are disproportionately investing more in the people and places that need more support, for example by expanding our targeted place-based working and partnerships.

While initial drops have stabilised for most groups, activity levels for the younger adults (16-34) have continued to fall at a worrying rate, continuing a downward trend that started before the pandemic. As the sport and physical activity sector recovers from coronavirus, it's vital that activity offerings appeal to this younger generation so they can benefit from the profound health, social and personal benefits that being active brings.

We'll also continue to work with Active Travel England, the government's agency, to improve cycling and walking infrastructure to make environments more suitable for the active travel with 51% of people saying they intend to do more walking, running or cycling for everyday journeys, which is likely to be linked to the cost of living crisis and rising fuel prices potentially making driving less accessible.

What happened to activity levels overall?

Our data shows that, between mid-November 2020 and mid-November 2021, just over six in 10 adults (28 million) achieved 150+ minutes of activity a week.

A further 11.5% (5.2m) were fairly active but didn't reach an average of 150 minutes a week, while 27.2% of people (12.4m) did less than an average of 30 minutes a week.

Unsurprisingly, activity levels reflected the level of restrictions in place at different stages of the pandemic.

There was a notable drop across mid-January to mid-March 2021 (which included a full national lockdown) compared to 12 months earlier. When restrictions eased, activity levels began to recover with increases seen across the summer compared to 12 months earlier.

Despite this, with the exception of mid-September to mid-November, activity levels remain below pre-pandemic levels (2019).

Types of activity being undertaken

Of those activities showing growth before the pandemic, only walking for leisure (+2.4m up to 24m) has continued to see numbers rise.

Active Travel – walking or cycling to get to a specific place – (-666k) and fitness activities (-1.3m) have both been notably impacted and seen large drops in numbers taking part.

However, 51% of people say they intend to do more walking, running or cycling for everyday journeys, which is likely to be linked to the cost of living crisis and rising fuel prices potentially making driving less accessible (Source: Savanta ComRes January 2022).

Cycling for leisure and sport (-784k) and running (-863k) have both seen numbers fall back since restrictions were eased in March 2021, following an initial rise.

Swimming (-354k) has seen a slight downward trend in numbers exacerbated by the pandemic with a large drop since November 2018-19.

The scale of the recovery

As the level of restrictions in place impacted activities in different ways, the scale of recovery has also differed by activity.

Despite no annual recovery, since mid-July (when all legal restrictions were lifted) team sport numbers have, largely, returned to pre-pandemic levels (2019).

Active travel numbers have seen a partial recovery from mid-March 2021 onwards whilst swimming numbers have started to recover since mid-May 2021.

Fitness activity numbers remain notably below pre-pandemic levels across the whole year (down 1.3m).

Demographic variations

Age

It remains the case that activity levels generally decrease with age, with those aged 16-34 (67%) most likely to be active, with the lowest activity levels for those age 75+ (to 39%).

Gender

Both men and women have seen a clear drop in activity levels compared to pre-pandemic (November 18-19), with levels stabilising over the last 12 months. The drops were slightly greater for men (down 2.2% or 376,000) than women (down 1.7% or 266,000).

Levels of activity

Summary of demographic differences

Our data shows there are significant inequalities

1 Gender

Men (63% or 14.0m) are more likely to be active than women (60% or 13.9m)

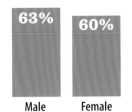

Male 63% | Female 60%

2 Socio-economic groups

Those in routine/ semi-routine jobs and those who are long-term unemployed or have never worked (NS-SEC 6-8*) are the least likely to be active (52%)

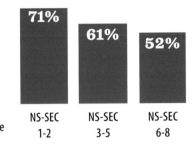

NS-SEC 1-2: 71% | NS-SEC 3-5: 61% | NS-SEC 6-8: 52%

NS-SEC groups are defined as:
- *Most affluent (NS-SEC 1-2): Managerial,administrative and professional occupations (e.g. chief executive, doctor, actor, journalist).*
- *Mid-affluent (NS-SEC 3-5): Intermediate, lower supervisory and technical occupations; self-employed and small employers (e.g. auxiliary nurse, secretary, plumber, gardener, train driver).*
- *Least affluent (NS-SEC 6-8): Semiroutine and routine occupations; longterm unemployed or never worked (e.g.post man, shop assistant, bus driver).*
- *Students and other (NS-SEC 9).*

3 Age

Activity levels genereally decrease with age, with the sharpest decrease coming at age 75+ (to 39%).

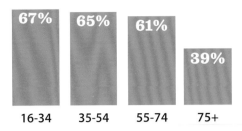

16-34: 67% | 35-54: 65% | 55-74: 61% | 75+: 39%

4 Disability and long-term health conditions

Activity is less common for disabled people or those with a long-term health condition* (45%) than those without (66%).

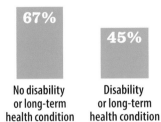

No disability or long-term health condition: 67% | Disability or long-term health condition: 45%

5 Ethnicity

There are differences in activity levels based on ethnic background

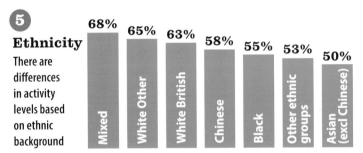

Mixed: 68% | White Other: 65% | White British: 63% | Chinese: 58% | Black: 55% | Other ethnic groups: 53% | Asian (excl Chinese): 50%

Source: Active Lives Adult Survey November 2020-21 Report
Published April 2022

Socio-economic groups

Activity levels among both the most and least affluent groups have seen a clear drop since the start of the pandemic in line with the national picture.

Ethnicity

Those with Mixed (68%), White British (63%) or White Other (65%) ethnicities remain more likely to be active than Chinese (58%), Black (55%) or Asian (excluding Chinese) (50%) people.

Disabled people and people with long-term health conditions

Activity levels for adults with a long-term health condition or a disability remain down compared to before the pandemic although their activity levels have stabilised over the last 12 months.

Our work through the pandemic

Throughout the pandemic, we've supported the sector with more than £270 million of funding, including our Community Emergency Fund and various Return to Play funding options that helped keep sports clubs and activity providers going through a very difficult period.

We've also managed the government's £600 million Sport Survival Package, that has supported organisations under severe financial pressure, and the £100 million National Leisure Recovery Fund to help public sector leisure centres to reopen to the public.

To tackle inequalities and support those most impacted by the restrictions, we made over £40 million of Tackling Inequalities Funding available and our campaigns Join the Movement, This Girl Can and We Are Undefeatable are continuing to help people stay active and provide guidance on how to find free, accessible activities.

In December, we launched our three-year plan that set out the steps we're taking to realise the ambitions in Uniting the Movement, and explained how we'll continue to give support where it's most needed as we help the sport and physical activity sector to recover and rebuild from Covid-19.

28th April 2022

Additional information
The Active Lives Adult Survey, which was established in November 2015, provides a world-leading approach to gathering data on how adults aged 16 and over in England engage with sport and physical activity.
The survey is conducted to provide decision-makers, government departments, local authorities, delivery bodies and the sport and physical activity sector detailed insight and understanding as to people's sport and physical activity habits.
It's carried out by leading research company IPSOS and produced by us in collaboration with the Office for Health Improvement and Disparities, the Department for Transport and Arts Council England.

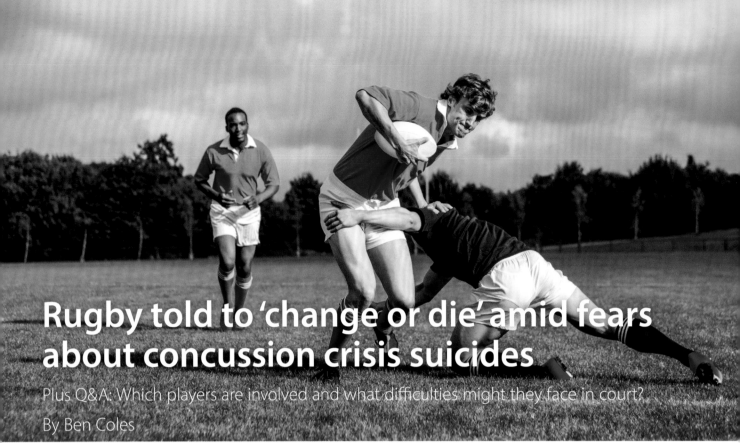

Rugby told to 'change or die' amid fears about concussion crisis suicides

Plus Q&A: Which players are involved and what difficulties might they face in court?

By Ben Coles

Rugby union has been warned it must change to protect its players 'otherwise the sport will die' after more than 185 players launched legal proceedings against World Rugby, the Rugby Football Union and Welsh Rugby Union.

Telegraph Sport can reveal new details of the lawsuit that was due to be filed at court on Monday on behalf of a group of professional and semi-professional players including Alix Popham, the former Wales international, as part of the biggest 'class action' lawsuit outside of the United States.

Popham, who was diagnosed with early onset dementia aged just 40 years old, has urged governing bodies to take immediate action to protect players from debilitating brain injuries after claiming they were negligent for failing to protect players.

Telegraph Sport can also reveal that the proceedings issued to the court by Rylands Law, representing the players, include:

♦ Players ranging from as young as their 20s to their 60s

♦ Another 50 players are going through testing or waiting for results with around two joining the legal proceedings every week

♦ Fears players will take their own lives if not supported

♦ Female players are now confirmed as part of the claimants

♦ As many as 'a few dozen' amateur rugby players are also involved

♦ Fears include how the NHS will cope with taking care of high numbers of retired professional athletes in middle age suffering from early onset dementia

Twenty players contacted brain charity Head For Change

after former Wales captain Ryan Jones revealed last week that he is suffering from early onset dementia, aged 41.

Health conditions among the group of claimants range from those suffering with more extreme cases of Motor Neurone Disease, Parkinson's and probably moderate Chronic Traumatic Encephalopathy (CTE), with the latter only confirmed following post-mortem.

The least extreme cases include players suffering from mild post-concussion syndrome, which can last for weeks, months or longer, while others in between suffer from epilepsy and the start of progressive neurodegenerative disease such as early onset dementia.

Symptoms include chronic depression, suicidal thoughts and attempts, aggression, addiction to alcohol and drugs as a result of their brain injuries, and a worsening memory and inability to concentrate.

'It's all pretty grim, to be honest, and quite consistent across the board,' said Richard Boardman, of Rylands Law.

'From our point of view, the ideal outcome is to get damages for the players and their young families to make sure they are looked after, and then ensure they have that clinical support in place. At the moment there is a considerable vacuum once a player has been diagnosed.

'The poor NHS is not set up for hundreds if not thousands of otherwise fit sportsmen in their 30s and 40s with dementia, in terms of how to deal with them.

'We're trying to work with foundations and charities and some kind clinicians who are helping us to ensure that we catch particularly the guys in the worst conditions, because they are in a bad way and they do need support. We don't want any of them to kill themselves.

'For this great sport to continue for another 100 years-plus, we have to accept that the brain is a delicate organ which needs heightened protection, and as a sport we have to err on the side of caution. Otherwise all brains, no matter what level you play at, are going to be impacted.'

Popham, now 42, won 33 caps for Wales but was diagnosed with early onset dementia 10 years after his retirement, when doctors estimated his brain had suffered up to 100,000 sub-concussions during 14 years of playing professionally. He now runs the brain charity Head For Change.

'There have been cases where I have spoken to family members of players who have taken their lives because of this,' Popham told Telegraph Sport, citing Wales' recent intense training sessions before their tour of South Africa as an example of how player welfare can improve.

'Rugby really needs to be reset and needs to be Rugby 2.0. The seasons need to be half what they are,' Popham added.

'There is a hell of a lot of evidence that contact sport has caused damage to players' brains. It's a terrible image for the sport, for mums and dads who are thinking of sending their kids to rugby there is a huge amount that needs to be changed to make it as safe as possible.

'For me, I still love rugby. We just need to draw a line in the sand with what has gone wrong. I'd have more respect for [World Rugby, RFU, WRU] if they put their hand up and said "yep, we made a mistake and here's what we are going to do now". Because otherwise the sport will die. And we don't want that.'

Progressive Rugby, the rugby union lobby group, also announced on Monday that they are in the process of 'finalising a comprehensive list of player welfare critical requirements which will be submitted to World Rugby'.

'We believe delay is no longer an option and that radical action must be taken as a matter of urgency to ensure rugby union's reputation isn't damaged beyond repair,' the group added. Those proposed changes include a mandatory limit on contact in training, improving pitchside diagnostic tools, reducing the number of non-injury substitutions, and extending the return-to-play for a concussion.

World Rugby, the RFU and WRU responded on Monday by saying: 'We care deeply about all our players, including former players, and never stand still when it comes to welfare. Our strategies to prevent, identify and manage head injuries are driven by a passion to safeguard our players and founded on the latest science, evidence and independent expert guidance.'

Q&A: Rugby's dementia crisis ends up in court
Who is involved?

More than 185 players are now part of the class action, including former Wales captain Ryan Jones who announced two weeks ago that he is suffering from early on-set dementia at the age of 41.

Other players involved include Steve Thompson, England's Rugby World Cup-winning hooker from 2003, who has said that he cannot remember winning the tournament.

When did preparations for the case begin?

Nine players, including Thompson and Popham and all under the age of 45, came together in December 2020 to propose legal proceedings against World Rugby, the Rugby Football Union in England and the Welsh Rugby Union.

What was the diagnosis for all those players involved?

All of the original nine claimants received the same diagnosis of dementia with probable chronic traumatic encephalopathy (CTE). The only known cause of CTE is repeated blows to the head, although CTE can only be confirmed following a post-mortem on the brain.

What has happened since the originally proposed legal proceedings?

Neither side has been able to agree on a settlement for the players involved, resulting in the matter going to court. The group litigation is set to become the biggest 'class action' outside of the United States, with the court now taking over the management of the cases, and legal proceedings are set to be issued against World Rugby, the RFU and WRU.

What have World Rugby, the RFU and WRU said?

All three governing bodies released a statement on Monday responding to the legal proceedings. 'We care deeply about all our players, including former players, and never stand still when it comes to welfare. Our strategies to prevent, identify and manage head injuries are driven by a passion to safeguard our players and founded on the latest science, evidence and independent expert guidance.'

How high could a potential settlement figure be?

'It's too early to say, but in a broad brush sense these are all pretty young men in early middle age with, many of them, progressive neurodegenerative brain injuries, so it's highly likely their claims would be considerable,' believes Richard Boardman of Rylands Law.

If the case went to court, how would it play out?

Jonathan Compton, partner at DMH Stallard, says: 'Where the claimants themselves will face difficulty is when they are asked specifically how they can attribute any of their conditions to their playing career, when did their symptoms start, how were they caused. But their sense that it is right to be seeking compensation seems just.

'For the governing bodies, when it comes to the matter possibly going to court, even if they were to win the optics do not look good. How would it come across asking former players suffering from health conditions to defend themselves in court?'

25 July 2022

More than 1 in 4 football and rugby union fans think not enough being done to prevent concussions in the professional game

With the impacts of concussion in professional sport becoming increasingly clear, do the public think enough is being done to tackle the problem?

By Keiran Pedley and Ben Roff

New research by Ipsos in the UK shows more than one in four football and rugby union fans do not think enough is being done to combat concussions in professional football and rugby union.

In a nationally representative poll of 2,051 British adults aged 16-75, Ipsos interviewed 921 football fans, 519 rugby union fans and 447 fans of cricket. In total, more than one in four football fans (28%) thought not enough was being done to prevent concussions in football. Meanwhile, 29% and 20% of rugby union and cricket fans thought not enough was being done in rugby union and cricket respectively.

However, overall more fans of each sport thought enough was currently being done with around one in four thinking that efforts to prevent concussions were actually going too far. For example:

♦ Among football fans, 45% thought the right amount was being done and 18% said too much. 28% said not enough.

♦ Among rugby union fans, 46% said the right amount was being done, 18% said too much and 29% said not enough.

♦ For cricket fans, 54% said the right amount was being done, 19% efforts were going too far and a roughly equal number (20%) said not enough was being done.

Keiran Pedley, Director of Research at Ipsos, said:

'These results show that whilst most football and rugby union fans think that either enough is being done to prevent concussions, or too much is being done, many think there is a problem. More than one in four supporters of both sports want to see more action taken to prevent concussions in the professional game, so the relevant authorities should not expect the pressure to act to disappear any time soon.'

Technical note:
Ipsos UK interviewed a representative quota sample of 2,051 adults aged 16-75 in Great Britain. 921 of the interviews were held with respondents who described themselves as football fans, 519 described themselves as rugby union fans and 447 described themselves as cricket fans. Interviews took place on the online Omnibus using the Ipsos.Digital platform on 5th April 2022. Data are weighted to match the profile of the population. All polls are subject to a wide range of potential sources of error.

6 May 2022

Is enough being done to prevent concussions in sports?

To what extent do you think to prevent concussions in the following professional sports have gone too far or not far enough, if either?

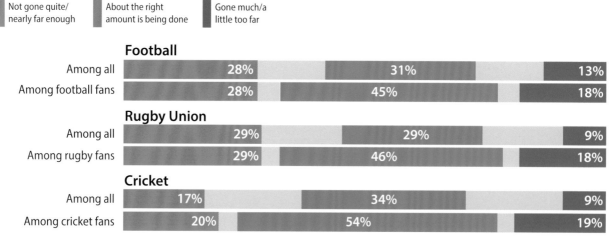

Legend: Not gone quite/nearly far enough | About the right amount is being done | Gone much/a little too far

Football
- Among all: 28% | 31% | 13%
- Among football fans: 28% | 45% | 18%

Rugby Union
- Among all: 29% | 29% | 9%
- Among rugby fans: 29% | 46% | 18%

Cricket
- Among all: 17% | 34% | 9%
- Among cricket fans: 20% | 54% | 19%

© IPSOS | May 2022

Base: 2,051 Online British adults aged 16-75 in Great Britain, including 921 Football fans, 519 Rugby Union fans, 447 Cricket fans 8-11th April 2022

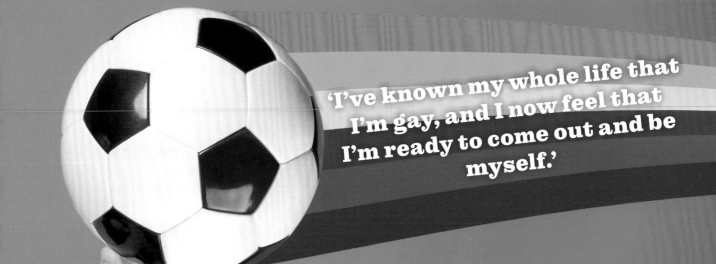

Jake Daniels' 21 words were momentous for football

Nathan O'Hagan explores what the 17-year-old Blackpool player's bravery in coming out publicly as gay will mean for other footballers and the game itself.

By Nathan O'Hagan

'I've known my whole life that I'm gay, and I now feel that I'm ready to come out and be myself.'

Twenty one simple words. The kind of words that are heard privately every day among friends and families, as a loved one chooses to reveal their truth to the most important people in their lives.

What is significant about these 21 words this week is that they were part of a public statement issued by Jake Daniels via his employer, Blackpool Football Club. By issuing this statement, Daniels became the first British professional footballer to publicly come out as gay in nearly four decades.

Given the number of people who have played the game professionally in this country in that time, it is inconceivable that there have not been other gay or bisexual players. The explanation is, of course, that while the law of averages clearly tells us that there have been many, the fact is that not one has felt empowered to state their sexuality publicly.

This is perhaps not surprising when you look at the first and – until this week – last player to do so.

Justin Fashanu was a prodigiously talented young player who began his career in 1978 with Norwich City. While at Norwich, he scored one of the most famous goals the

English game has ever seen – a sumptuous turn and volley against Liverpool which was so good it graced the opening credits of Match of the Day for years afterwards.

In 1980, Fashanu became the first black player to be sold for £1 million when he moved from Norwich to Nottingham Forest. It was at Forest that perceptions of his sexuality first began to negatively impact his career.

Although not publicly out, many of his teammates were aware he was gay. His visiting of Nottingham's gay clubs came to the attention of manager Brian Clough, who labelled him a 'bloody poof' and banned him from training with the first team squad.

Despite his talent, Fashanu's career quickly went off the rails and he spent most of the next decade on short-term contracts and loans in the lower leagues and in America and Canada. He officially came out in 1990 when a British newspaper threatened to out him. Fashanu eventually took his own life in a lock-up in Shoreditch in 1998 after being accused of sexual assault in the US.

It's more than 30 years since Fashanu came out and, given the hostility he suffered – with even his brother, fellow-pro John Fashanu, describing him as 'an outcast' in The Voice newspaper – it is perhaps unsurprising that since then the only other high-profile case is that of Thomas Hitzlsperger, the former West Ham, Aston Villa and Everton midfielder who came out in 2014.

The significant difference between these two examples and Daniels, however, is that Fashanu's career was well into its third act. He came out in 1990, a year in which he spent time playing at Leyton Orient in the old third division and in Canada with Hamilton Steelers. Germany international Hitzlsperger was the most high-profile player to come out, but even he did so a year after he retired from the game.

The only other modern comparison is Josh Carvalho, a midfielder with Adelaide United in Australia's A League, who came out last year at the age of 21. Carvalho remains the only out footballer playing in the top division of his country.

Jake Daniels, meanwhile, is just 17 years old – barely taking the first kicks of his footballing journey. He will have to deal with any potential negative response, as well as the weight of responsibility that comes with being a trailblazer, at an age when most of us are still figuring out a way to not be late for school or work.

It takes a special kind of strength and resolve to succeed in professional football at any level – to attempt to do so with the added weight and scrutiny that Daniels will now be subject to marks him out as an especially courageous individual.

The timing of his statement is also significant for the game itself.

Undeniable progress has been made in attitudes and behaviours on the terraces in recent times. The Rainbow Laces campaign has been active for several years, for instance, and clubs have made efforts to give a voice to LGBTQ fan groups. But, despite these small but significant steps, there was one glaring omission – the lack of a professional player willing to come out publicly.

This is in contrast to the women's professional game, where representation is far better. At the 2019 Women's World Cup, for example, there were more than 40 gay or bisexual players and coaches, compared with a grand total of zero at the men's equivalent the year before.

FIFA must take some responsibility for this. While it has publicly made the right noises in support of LGBTQ fans and of Jake Daniels' statement, it chose Russia – a country with many anti-gay laws – as the host for the 2018 World Cup. Meanwhile, this year's tournament in December will be held in Qatar, a country where male homosexuality is illegal and punishable by up to three years in prison.

As with its past ineptitude when dealing with racist incidents, so far the game's governing body has yet to prove with actions that it can be counted on as an ally for gay players.

For all these reasons, how momentous Daniels' statement was this week cannot be overstated. There will be numerous other gay footballers quietly watching from the touchline to see how this plays out – many of them will have been in the game for years and may now have been shown the way by a teenager in the nascent stages of his career.

Quite where that career will take Daniels at this point remains to be seen. But, if he approaches the rest of it with the bravery he has shown this week, then he could well go on to achieve great things. Whatever he does on the pitch, Jake Daniels' place in footballing history is already assured.

20 May 2022

Netball is the growing sport trend for women of all ages – including those over 50

Whether you played centre, goal attack or wing defence, most of us girls will remember playing netball during our school years.

By Vicki-Marie Cossar

However, while many of us haven't played since then, the sport has had some really positive growth recently.

Before the pandemic, netball was increasing in popularity and participation levels were at an all-time high.

England Netball, the national governing body responsible for the strategic plan for netball across the country, report that around 685,000 women and girls were taking to courts across the country in a typical week during the season.

England's netball squad, the Vitality Roses, are ranked third in the world and since they won gold at the Commonwealth Games in April 2018, participation levels in netball have risen.

In fact, more than 160,000 Brits took up the game after the Vitality Netball World Cup in July 2020, according to YouGov data, and there was a significant increase in those aged 55 to 74-years-old taking part.

It is the second largest team sport for women after football and there are lots of reasons why playing netball is a brilliant workout.

The ASICS Uplifting Minds study found that stopping exercise for a week has the same effect on your mental wellbeing as seven nights of broken sleep, with significant falls in areas including confidence levels, energy and ability to cope with stress.

If you're not a fan of the gym, or home exercise, signing up for a weekly game of netball (or any sporting activity for that matter) could help prevent this decline.

The study also found that just 15 minutes and nine seconds is enough to significantly improve our state of mind and, with a game of netball split into four, 15-minute quarters, it can be uplifting even if you can't play a full game.

For anyone who might need a recap, netball is typically played by two teams of seven and involves players passing a ball up and down a court while defending and attacking.

The aim is to shoot the ball through your opponent's net, which stands on a 10ft-high metal post.

Players have to stick to specific zones on the court and once the ball is caught, you can only pivot with the ball. It's fast-paced and skill, agility, balance and tactics are of the essence.

'decreased depressive symptoms in some by as much as 70%) and it works well on anxiety,' she says.

According to Women In Sport, the top motivators for women aged 36-55 participating in netball were enjoyment and mental wellbeing but also physical health, too. So what fitness benefits can you expect?

'Sprint, jump, land and pivot are the basic fundamentals that make up netball,' explains Tom McClelland, UK head of athletic training at Virgin Active.

'The game itself is demanding and most of these movements are powered by the anaerobic system.

'Physically speaking, with all the jumping, landing and footwork, netball is a full-body workout that builds muscle, makes bones stronger and improves cardio fitness, balance and coordination. Just remember that mobility and recovery after a game are important. Foam-rolling, self-massage and stretching are crucial, especially if you haven't played for a while.'

'Don't let your busy life stand in the way of the game'

Sophia Candappa plays semi-professionally for Surrey Storm.

The 29-year-old also holds down a full-time job as a teacher (currently on maternity leave) and has two children aged two-and-a-half and five months.

'I've been playing netball since I was about ten,' she says.

'I started at school, then joined a local club and went semi-pro at university.

'In season I dedicate about 12 hours a week to netball, with team training twice a week and a game at the weekend, but I do strength and conditioning training every day, too. It's a big commitment but I love playing.

'I love the camaraderie. It's a fun environment but also challenging.

'For me it's about time management. I plan the week ahead with the family and I prioritise training time and block it out in my diary. It's not easy, though – the juggle is real.

'I'm often tired but when I get to training it's exactly what I needed in terms of seeing people and getting the endorphins flowing.'

14 April 2022

At the highest level, there are 11 teams which form the Vitality Netball Superleague, with nine from England, one from Scotland and one from Wales.

For everyday folk, there are approximately 3,500 member netball clubs across England with programmes on offer including Back To Netball, for those who haven't played for a while and need a fun and friendly reintroduction to the sport, Walking Netball, a slower version of the game for all ages and abilities, and Netball Now, which are non-coached sessions where you just turn up and play.

'School team sports can feel a bit Marmite in our memories: some love the camaraderie, others vividly remember being the last to be picked,' says Dr Josephine Perry, a sport psychologist and founder of Performance In Mind.

'When children are asked in surveys why they play sports, the number one answer is always "to have fun".

'Yet we know girls start dropping out of sport aged only seven and one of the biggest reasons given is that having fun gets overtaken by a feeling that they are supposed to want to win. It becomes all about competition.

'As adults, team games can be far more inclusive, much less bitchy, and expectation levels kinder. This makes them a great option for dipping your toe back into fitness in a way that can feel more like socialising than sport.'

Dr Josephine explains that as adults we often start sports because we want to get fitter and healthier, but we stay because we enjoy being part of the team, we value the coping mechanisms we learn, the brilliant friends we make and the boost to our confidence.

We also discover there are mental and cognitive benefits we struggle to get elsewhere.

'When you find a source of exercise that works for you it changes the way you process and respond to your emotions, reduces overthinking, and builds up emotional resilience to stress. Mentally it can be as effective as anti-depressants at helping reduce symptoms of depression (one study found it

Women's sports are more popular than ever – so why are there only three statues of female athletes in the UK?

An article from The Conversation.

By Chris Stride, Senior Lecturer (Statistician), University of Sheffield

Since the ancient Greeks and their Olympians, statues have been a way to commemorate athletic achievement. In recent decades, the global inventory of sporting monuments has grown to include a wide range of sports. There is no rulebook governing which athletes deserve commemoration – but those chosen for such an honour can tell us much about the values and priorities of modern sporting culture.

One notable theme in sports statuary is how few statues there are of women. The sporting statues project database has recorded statues around the world of more than 750 different football players and managers – but only seven are from the women's game – and all were erected in the past decade. This includes the current England women's coach, Sarina Wiegman, who is Dutch, at the Netherlands football HQ in Zeist.

The US has more than 300 baseball statues, yet only two are of female players. Across the UK, of the 220 sportspeople who have been honoured by statues, only three are women. Dorothy Round, twice Wimbledon ladies singles winner in the 1930s, is commemorated in her home town of Dudley. Dame Mary Peters won Olympic gold in the pentathlon in 1972 – her statue now overlooks the Belfast athletics track that bears her name. Lily Parr was the goal-scoring star of the boom in women's football following the first world war. Her sculpture was commissioned by the National Football Museum in Manchester and unveiled in 2019.

An immediate and cynical reaction to this would be to assume that organisations, groups and sponsors who organise and pay for these monuments have a deeply misogynistic streak. But I don't think this is the case. The lack of statues of sportswomen does reflect discrimination, but not necessarily in the discussions about choosing who to honour with a statue. Rather, it is a symptom of historical marginalisation of women within sport, the sports most

likely to have their heroes cast in bronze, and the motivations of sports organisations, civic authorities and fans when erecting a new statue.

Team sports players are far more likely to receive a statue than athletes within individual sports. Of the UK's 220 subject-specific sports statues, almost half depict footballers (106), with rugby players (15) or cricketers (10) also featuring regularly. Team sports organisations such as football clubs have money to pay for statues, land to erect them on, and the fan base to campaign for them. They also have a variety of motivations for commissioning a statue, such as increasing fan attachment through nostalgia and a sense of their club's authenticity, or giving their shiny new stadium a sense of club-specific visual identity.

In the UK and elsewhere, women have historically faced resistance to their participation in the most popular team sports. For example, between 1921 and 1971, the Football Association banned women's teams from playing at FA-affiliated football grounds. Therefore, the sports most likely to have statues of their heroes are the very same sports in which female participants have been marginalised. And, even when they do take part, women are starved of the professional competition and media coverage that could elevate them to popular heroes.

Where are the statues of sportswomen?

While women's team sports have received a much higher profile in the past decade, this hasn't boosted the numbers of sportswomen with statues. This is likely due to the influence of fan nostalgia when selecting statue subjects. Sport statues are as much about memory as history – famous athletes who retired 20-30 years ago are the most likely to be honoured. This works against our current barrier-breaking women's footballers, whose exploits are too recent to generate a sense of nostalgia.

On the other hand, there are far fewer statues depicting legends from individual sports, due to the lack of a cohesive club-centric infrastructure and fan base. Where such statues do exist, they are most likely to feature combatants from the more dangerous sports, such as motor racing (22 such statues in the UK) and boxing (16 UK statues and many more worldwide). These sports generate a strong sense of community within their participants and fans. They also often have an additional motivation to erect a statue – the death of a competitor. The small village of Ballymoney, Northern Ireland, has sculptures of three champion motorcycling members of the Dunlop family, all killed in action while road racing.

As with team sports, there have been historic barriers to female participation in such risky individual events, reducing the probability of a female statue subject. The first woman received a UK licence to box professionally in 1998 and only a handful of women have ever raced in an F1 grand prix.

The events in which women have had more opportunities to display their talent in front of large crowds and seep into popular culture are non-dangerous individual sports – notably athletics, swimming, equestrianism and tennis. Overall, there are relatively fewer statues of competitors from individual sports as compared to team sports, regardless of gender. When they do exist, however, there is less bias against women as statue subjects.

Globally, and in the UK, there are roughly equal numbers of statues of male and female tennis players. Around the world there are more statues of male track and field athletes, but female athletes make up between 25% and 30% of subjects, reflecting the smaller proportion of Olympic events they have historically been able to compete in (until 1972, the longest distance race open to women was the 800m). This suggests that, where women's sport has been elevated to a level similar to equivalent men's events, heroes have emerged that the public want to celebrate, and their gender is not counting against them being monumentalised.

The lack of statues of female athletes should make us think about the merits of sporting achievements. Heroic performances, popular acclaim and nostalgic sentiment are often placed above pioneering organisational work, breaking down barriers and inspiring others. Breaking the 'bronze ceiling' calls for a change in these priorities.

6 July 2022

The mystery of testosterone and women's sport

Leading scientist labels the IOC's focus on hormones in trans women as 'simplistic' and a 'mess'.

By Fiona Thomas

When sports scientist Dave Hamilton set out to monitor the testosterone levels of an international women's hockey team it was with the aim of measuring how the athletes were coping with their new heavier training load. Hamilton took three weeks' worth of daily salivary samples from the players, one in the morning and one in the afternoon after physical activity. The study did not throw up any red flags around their training schedules, but it did yield some unexpected results.

'What we found was that relative to a sedentary population, [the women] had high testosterone levels,' said Hamilton, who now works in a similar high-performance role at Tampa Bay Buccaneers. 'We also found the people who were on oral contraception, versus those who weren't, had lower testosterone levels.' In fact, women who weren't on oral contraception had testosterone concentrations that were on average 35 per cent higher than those who were on the pill.

It is an intriguing insight into the diverse levels of testosterone among sportswomen. In an age where the 'T' word has become the centre of a fierce debate around whether trans and differences in sex development (DSD) athletes should be allowed to compete in women's sport – with testosterone levels often the determining factor – the hormone is often misunderstood as having an impact exclusive to men.

Much of the lack of understanding stems back to the historical underinvestment in sports science research on women.

Unlike the current testosterone trans policies in sport, which measure levels in the blood, Hamilton's study focused on the salivary or 'free' testosterone, which yields a much smaller amount of the hormone. The findings uncovered sharp changes in response to a diverse range of stimuli - from exercise and music, to coaching feedback, sleep, being in a group setting or on your own.

'We guided our programme knowing that testosterone responds to a physical and also an environmental stress,' explained Hamilton. 'There's been a lot of research that shows when you win, testosterone levels go up, when you lose, testosterone levels go down. If you think a regular female sits around 20 to 40 pg/ml of free testosterone, you could go from a recording of 25 to 55 pg/ml.'

There was, however, another significant finding. 'We had a large portion of our team reporting testosterone levels in the range of 80 to 100pg/ml, which is in line with the average male level of testosterone,' said Hamilton. 'There was also nothing in our data to suggest that if 'x' had the highest T levels she was the best athlete. That just wasn't a thing.'

On the contrary, high testosterone levels in athletic female populations – entering male ranges – have been found previously, as demonstrated by a 2014 study published in the *Journal of Clinical Endocrinology*.

Based on blood samples of 693 athletes, the study found that 16.5 per cent of men had low testosterone levels, whereas 13.7 per cent of women had high levels, with a complete overlap between the sexes. The paper criticised the International Olympic Committee's then definition of normal testosterone levels for a woman as 'untenable'.

'There are a lot of men with low testosterone who are good athletes,' said Peter Sonksen, an Emeritus professor in endocrinology at St Thomas' Hospital and King's College, London, who co-led the study and whose research for the International Olympic Committee eventually led to the development of an anti-doping test for Human Growth Hormone.

'And there are a lot of women with very high testosterone who are also good athletes. The simple issue is always that testosterone makes them super athletes, but that's b-------.'

Can testosterone make you a 'super-athlete'?

The issue is so complex and polarising that - largely due to a lack of data - the IOC now allows global sporting federations to determine their own trans policies. It had previously recommended that trans women suppress testosterone levels to under 10 n/mol per litre for at least 12 months in order to compete, meanwhile the Union Cycliste Internationale stipulates cyclists must keep below a level of 5 nmol/L for a period of at least 12 months. 'It's an incredibly sensitive area and one where they're being deliberately simplistic and messing up the science,' added Sonksen.

The IOC defended its approach towards the 'evolving topic' of trans women in sport and highlighted how new studies have not provided a consensus on how testosterone affects performance across all sports. It added: 'There is no single right answer from science at this stage as the scientific evidence needs to be specific to each sport or discipline and how competitive advantage is to be measured there.'

So minute is the trans women population that, nearly two decades after the IOC originally mandated trans athletes could compete in the Olympics providing they underwent gender reassignment surgery, sport is still in the early stages of its fact-finding mission to understand whether trans women in sport possess an advantage over cis women. At the heart of the debate - which intensified earlier this month after trans cyclist Emily Bridges was barred from riding in the National Omnium Championships - is testosterone.

'There is going to be some advantage'

One study published last year in the British Journal of Sports Medicine found that trans women who underwent hormone therapy for one year continued to maintain an athletic advantage, despite a 15-31 per cent decline in physical performance.

Based on transgender men and women serving in the US military, it found the 15–31 per cent athletic advantage trans women displayed over their cis women counterparts prior to starting gender affirming hormones declined with feminising therapy. However, trans women still had a nine percent faster mean run speed after one year of testosterone suppression.

'It becomes a discussion of how low, for how long,' says Dr Christina Marie Roberts, a paediatrician and associate professor at the University of Missouri-Kansas City who led the research. She points to a variation that exists among cis gender women, which has flown under the radar in the context of discussing fairness in sport.

'The IOC originally picked 10 nmol/l because that's the highest naturally occurring levels of testosterone in women. Some women with PolyCystic Ovarian Syndrome will have higher levels of testosterone than other women. Testosterone, wherever it's coming from, is an advantage, so there is going to be some advantage in women's sport anyway.'

Competing in the mixed-gender sport of motor racing, Charlie Martin - the British racing driver who hopes to become the first transgender driver to compete in the Le Mans 24 hours - believes understanding of testosterone in trans women is often misunderstood. Having undergone a medical transition, which included full gender reassignment surgery, her body does not produce testosterone in any real quantity. 'It's simple stuff like that which most people don't think about,' says Martin, in reference to the debate about whether trans women should compete in female sport.

She adds: 'I'd say my strength is in line with that of a cis gender woman who does a similar amount of training to me and eats and trains well. That's my experience and the experience of pretty much every trans woman I know.'

Leading the research in this country, is an ongoing study - in which Bridges is participating - at Loughborough University. Dr Emma O'Donnell, a senior lecturer in exercise physiology there, highlights the challenges of the work. 'With such a small transgender athlete population to draw from, and the variations in the physiological demands of different sporting disciplines, unfortunately it will be some years before we have the data required to inform sporting bodies to allow them to create evidence-based guidelines regarding transgender sport participation.'

O'Donnell says that testosterone remains a vital element to the study. 'Testosterone is an important parameter to consider,' said O'Donnell. 'Testosterone levels increase almost 20 fold during male puberty, marking a time of significant physiological change in males. The testosterone exposure that an adult trans woman will have been exposed to before commencing testosterone-lowering hormone therapy is therefore an important consideration when trying to understand the effects of hormone therapy on athletic performance.' At this time, these effects remain unclear.

28 April 2022

A big day for women's rugby

Fairness and safety should be upheld.

By Fiona Thomas

On Friday the Rugby Football Union Council will vote on whether to restrict women's rugby to those born female. Given that rugby is a full-contact sport with a concussion problem, you'd think it obvious that heavier, stronger, faster male bodies should not be tackling women, no matter how those male bodies identify.

It's more than two years since World Rugby made the case, putting female safety ahead of the wishes of trans-identifying males for validation, based on the increased concussion risk for females in a clash with a male body. Thankfully, it looks like the RFU is about to do the right thing and follow World Rugby in limiting the women's game to those born female, albeit two seasons later. We congratulate them on having the integrity to recognise the need for policy change and to act on it.

Fair Play For Women has been lobbying the RFU and national governing bodies of other sports (NGBs) for years now, pointing out that women and girls are adversely affected if they lose their female-only teams, events and competitions. Often the answer has been that there are

'only a few transwomen'. But just one transwoman in a league affects dozens, sometimes hundreds, of female players. Anyone who feels compassion for those trans players and their wish to play the game they love should consider the impact on females who have the same wish.

'Their daughters are playing a game with some risk'

We have heard from match referees who are afraid they will see a woman seriously injured on their watch, because they are not allowed to question whether an obviously-male player belongs on the field. We've heard from worried parents of young female rugby players. They know their daughters are playing a game with some risk, but if a teenage girl finds herself tackling — or worse, being tackled by — a teenage boy, it's a whole different ball game. That's before you factor in the girls' embarrassment at sharing changing rooms or showers with an intact male.

Until now, those parents and referees could not object. They were advised that a transgirl is a girl and they must not comment. To point out that by definition a transgirl has a male body could mean the end of their involvement in rugby. We are relieved and delighted to see the RFU tackle this issue and, we hope, reinstate fairness and safety for their female players when they vote.

Recent policy changes by the international swimming federation FINA and the UK governing body British Triathlon show that common sense is returning. But some governing bodies such as British Cycling and the English Cricket Board are resisting. Despite being forced to withdraw their transgender inclusion policy in April this year, British Cycling, backed by cycling's international federation UCI, is clinging to the discredited idea of testosterone suppression as the basis on which a person who's been through the myriad changes wrought by male puberty can compete against females, who have not.

Meanwhile, males are still racing and taking titles, podium places, cash prizes and ranking points in women's cycling in the UK. We know of one who has taken regional championships and medals at national level, and another who's taken podium places in a range of cycling disciplines.

'Dozens have been affected'

It's easy to think this isn't happening, because the results list female names. But each of these cyclists who have male performance advantage are displacing women, pushing them down the results, every time they race. Dozens have been affected by just a few trans competitors — and that is since the British Cycling policy was supposedly suspended.

Cricket has not bothered with the fig leaf of testosterone suppression, saying anyone who identifies as a woman can play in a women's team. It is not unusual for such players to be in both men's and women's teams, though their batting average is always much better when they play women, helped by the shorter boundary of the women's game.

There are injury risks in cricket too, where more skilled players bowl faster and hit harder, leaving other players, especially wicket keepers, open to injury. The ECB's response to Fair Play For Women is that they are piloting a 'disparity policy', giving umpires the power to remove a player where there is such a disparity of skill that they may represent a risk to others on the pitch.

The disparity policy is not about trans players. It's to address skill differences between, say, elite men and club-level men. It's not clear whether this pilot even includes any teams with trans players in them. It's hard to imagine an umpire daring to remove a trans player during a match under this policy. Is it because they are trans? Or is it because they are male? One suspects either reason would be deemed transphobic.

Women's sport has come a long way, with equal representation at the Olympics, but female participation at grassroots still lags far behind that of men. While the Sports Councils and many NGBs have specific targets and funding to increase female participation, they have adopted 'inclusive' policies which are leading to females being excluded or self-excluding.

Last year the UK's Sports Council Equality Group published revised guidance stating that trans inclusion in female sport was incompatible with fairness, and in some sports safety, for females. Polling published last week by YouGov shows that the British public understand that it is not fair for females to have to share the pitch or the pool or the track with males, because sport is about sexed bodies not identities. We know it, the sports councils know it, the general public know it. Sports governing bodies must know it too.

27 July 2022

Women in sport are winning the fight for equal pay – slowly

An article from The Conversation.

THE CONVERSATION

By Beth Clarkson, Senior Lecturer in Sports Management, University of Portsmouth, Alex Culvin, Senior Lecturer in Sports Business, Leeds Beckett University & Ali Bowes, Senior Lecturer in Sociology of Sport, Nottingham Trent University

The Welsh national football association has pledged to introduce equal pay for their men's and women's teams by 2026. The news comes following a documentary featuring the most capped Welsh player Jess Fishlock, who called the lack of pay parity 'unacceptable'.

It also follows the Irish football association's introduction of pay parity for its national teams. Through a combination of the men's squad agreeing to reduce their international fees, and the association matching their contribution, all players will now receive €2,000 per match. Wales and Ireland join England, Brazil, Australia, Norway and New Zealand as national football associations who have equal pay agreements with men's and women's teams.

These recent cases are indicative of real change in how some national governing bodies view women's sport, long considered 'less than' the men's versions and chronically underfunded. And, as these bodies are social institutions – their decisions and financial support influence how society views sport – this is good news for women's sport more broadly. However, for many players and athletes, progress is slow and challenges remain.

For years, a lack of pay has left many women navigating a complex balancing act of elite level sport and work or study. Many continue to do so. Sportswomen, despite making professional commitments and complying to professional expectations, are often treated as amateurs.

However, many women athletes have been reluctant to question inadequate workplace conditions as there is often a 'be grateful' narrative enveloping women in professional sport environments. Yet, to acquire professional status offers legitimacy to women athletes.

Pay across the pond

Perhaps the highest-profile challenge for equal pay in football comes from the US women's national team, who has had long, unrivalled success on the international stage. Yet for the past five years, their highly publicised legal battle – and the 'equal play, equal pay' campaign – has drawn attention to the lack of pay parity in the sport.

Although the dispute started in 2016, in 2019, the team took the US Soccer Federation to court in pursuit of better pay and working conditions. At the time, an economic expert noted the women's team could be owed US$66 million (£48.2 million).

US Soccer has fought against the case on multiple grounds, made more complex by the fact that both parties are using different sets of statistics to attempt to prove or disprove the team's financial success. Both parties also disagree about the performance comparisons with the men's team, with US Soccer controversially arguing -– although later backtracking -– that in football, men do different work to women.

The US team's initial complaints were dismissed, as they were unable to prove a breach of the Equal Pay Act. In our recent research, we analysed the implications of the US women's team's collective action lawsuit against US Soccer, highlighting the need for formal, legal reform, such as Iceland's Equal Pay Certification. The new legislation contains amendments to the 2008 'Gender Equality Act' which aims to reduce gender-based pay discrimination.

Professional women footballers operate in a more precarious workplace, with poorer conditions, lower pay, shorter contracts and a smaller number of professional opportunities than men. As explained in our analysis of the USWNT dispute, this is a by-product of decades of gendered discrimination.

US Soccer has since offered the same pay structure to all its senior players, but the women's team believe the offer does not go far enough if it means a reduction in player earnings. The legal case is still ongoing, with the team filing an appeal this summer after a judge dismissed their lawsuit.

Women's football has arguably led the way in the fight for equal pay, but there have also been notable changes in rugby in recent months. England's women have risen to the top of the world rankings since fully professionalising at the start of 2019. This year, an under-fire Welsh Rugby Union offered women rugby players professional contracts. Although there are still issues to be overcome, for the first time in their history up to ten players will have full-time professional contracts, with a further 15 players on retainer contracts.

While the increase in both professional opportunities and pay parity for women athletes is worthy of celebration, women should not have to feel grateful for the opportunity. And, like the USWNT have done so publicly, they can legitimately demand, and expect, more.

29 November 2021

The FA Cup must close its gender pay gap, a prize pot 70 times less than the men is shameful

The FA spending more on prize money would be so much more valuable for society, as a message of equality, than any 'gameplan for growth'.

By Tom Garry, women's football reporter

Of course the pledge to address the gender pay gap is a welcome move from the governing body - after mounting pressure and widespread protests from fans - but the women's game as a whole should be reserving judgement until some hard numbers are made public.

This is not about equal pay. I have never heard anybody in women's football ask for equal salaries to their male counterparts in the Premier League or the EFL. Rather, this is about prize money - something the FA can control.

The FA have an opportunity to send out a very powerful message to women's football around the world, that the game is truly valued. To give women's winners the same prize money as men's winners would send such a positive message that men and women are treated equally.

And yes, it's true, the men's competition attracts far larger audiences, greater commercial revenue streams and has bigger salaries to pay. But comparing the men's and women's games, like-for-like in 2022 is nonsensical given that men's football was not banned by the FA for five decades.

When sports broadcaster Shebahn Aherne suggested on TalkSport on Friday that the FA should compensate women's football for that ban, former Crystal Palace chairman Simon Jordan quickly dismissed the suggestion as 'silly'. But the truth is that the FA do still owe the women's game, regardless of their impressive investments in the modern era.

Even if prize money were made equal, teams in the men's FA Cup would still earn more money from broadcast revenues, and income from sponsorship would still be higher. Those are factors driven by market demand. But the FA can decide, of its own accord, how to spend its own money on prize funds.

To their credit, the FA do invest many millions into women's football each year. But spending more of those on Women's FA Cup prize money would be so much more valuable for society, as a message of equality, than any 'gameplan for growth'. The magic of The FA Cup? For now, at least, not so much.

Ole Gunnar Solskjaer and his wife Silje watched from the stands as their daughter Karna made her senior debut for Manchester United against Bridgwater United.

The 19-year-old forward, who plays in the academy at the same club her father managed and fired to Champions League glory as a player, was brought on as an 87th-minute substitute as her side eased into the fifth round.

'It wasn't a token for Karna, it was a deserved [debut], from the performance that I saw from her the other day. So congratulations to her,' said head coach Marc Skinner, who had watched Wednesday's 5-0 win for Manchester United's under-21s in the Academy Cup semi-finals against Aston Villa.

Karna scored and impressed in front of her father and Skinner added: 'Obviously she's got a famous dad, but she wants to be famous in her own right.'

The band of travelling fans sang 'you are my Solskjaer' when Karna was finally brought on.

Skinner, whose senior side have now won seven straight games without conceding thanks to their controlled, 2-0 win, underlined the close bond between the Solskjaer family and Manchester United, adding: 'We were privileged to have Ole as our manager, as well as a wonderful player for this club, but again, it stops becoming about Ole as much, and more about Karna. It's so important that we raise that fact.

'And maybe, if we are talking about the beauty and the romanticism of the FA Cup, maybe this is a story of the romanticism of the Solskjaers and how important they are to this club.'

And just as it was a day that the Solskjaer family will never forget in the Somerset sunshine, the cup tie will live long in the memory of Bridgwater too, as they smashed their club record crowd and attracted around 10 times their third-tier women's team's average league attendance.

And the hosts certainly did not disgrace themselves, defending valiantly to stay in the game for long periods against the team third in the top flight, but Charlotte Buxton's early own goal and Ella Toone's clinical 80th-minute finish eventually sealed victory.

There was not a single spare vantage point in the ground and the match had the feel of a classic FA Cup encounter. The opener saw defender Buxton inadvertently turn the ball into her own net under pressure from Wales's Hayley Ladd from Ivana Fuso's 17th-minute cross and, after long spells of Manchester United possession and dominance of territory, England forward Toone found the bottom corner.

Sitting fourth in the southern section of English women's football's third tier, Bridgwater were always huge underdogs but Skinner – who named a strong team – added: 'I hope today has created a lot of opportunity for players at Bridgwater and in the surrounding area. It reminds you of the wonder of English football.'

31 January 2022

The lack of girls' football in schools is shameful, Ian Wright was spot on

Huge numbers of young Lionesses fans won't have a football club to join in September – the gap in access between boys and girls is shocking.

By Katherine Lucas

Ian Wright could have been lost in the moment, while most of the nation was still lost in wonder at Alessia Russo.

While Sweet Caroline was ringing around Bramall Lane, nobody was thinking 'what a state girls' football is in this country'. There was no-one dwelling on how few girls will actually get to play football when this summer of celebration ends and they go back to school in September.

As Ellen White roared her way around the edge of the pitch, none of the fans she greeted were contemplating how unlikely this story was for the older players in this squad; that as youngsters, White, Luzy Bronze and Fran Kirby would not have even bothered to dream of playing in a sold-out European Championship final at Wembley.

But it is a conversation that has to happen. Wright was precisely the right person to raise it, because he has been so invested in women's football long before it captured a peak audience of more than nine million people on Tuesday night.

'Whatever happens in the final now, if girls are not allowed to play football in their PE – just like the boys can – what are we doing?' he said.

'We have got to make sure they are able to play and get the opportunity to do so. If there's no legacy to this – like with the Olympics – then what are we doing, as this is as proud as I've ever felt of any England side.'

Until he spoke on BBC, many won't have been aware that this was even an issue. Predictably, Wright's comments were met with some of the anecdotalism that can so often be used to trivialise. 'I know at least two girls who play football on Saturdays', and 'when I was at school even 20 years ago, there was a girls' team'.

All those things can be true, but they do not necessarily reflect the wider reality. Just 40 per cent of secondary schools in the UK offer girls the same access to football via after-school clubs as boys.

In schools as a whole, only 63 per cent offer girls the chance to play football as much as the boys in P.E. The numbers are even worse in secondary school; it's 72 per cent in primary school, but 44 per cent from Year 7 onwards.

The FA hope that by 2024, 75 per cent of grassroots clubs will offer at least one girls' team. Programmes like 'Wildcats' are hoping to engage more female coaches and players at all levels. English football's governing bodies want another 120,000 girls to be given the chance to play football, and they expect that within two years' time, 75 per cent of schools will provide equal access.

Some of the FA's targets are even more ambitious, like a rapid increase in the number of female referees and ensuring England win a major tournament by 2024 – that means either this summer's Euros, with just one more hurdle to go, or next year's World Cup in Australia and New Zealand. Yet what Wright was talking about goes beyond the now instantly recognisable 23-player squad picked by Sarina Wiegman.

Nor is it just about attendances and viewing figures for the Women's Super League next season.

It's making sure the little girl pictured in full England kit singing long after the final whistle does not end up with no club to play for, or losing interest because she can't play football with her school friends.

It's making sure girls of primary school age aren't caught in a vicious cycle where they are taught exclusively by teachers who themselves were restricted to netball and athletics.

Imagine the number of girls who will be gasping to kick a ball if Wiegman's side are crowned European champions on Sunday. As it stands, around a quarter of them won't be able to.

'We said before the tournament and throughout that we want to inspire the nation,' Wiegman said after England had beaten Sweden 4-0.

'I think that's what we're doing and making a difference. The whole country is proud of us and even more girls and boys will want to play football.'

27 July 2022

Sexism and sport: why body-baring team uniforms are bad for girls and women

An article from The Conversation.

THE CONVERSATION

By Sarah Zipp, University of Stirling, Sasha Sutherland, The University of the West Indies, Barbados and Lilamani de Soysa, University of Tsukuba

Team outfits and fashion were not supposed to be a big talking point at the 2020 Olympics in Tokyo. But protests over skimpy uniforms by two women's teams in the months before the games have brought bikinis and high-cut leotards into the spotlight. Now these high-profile campaigns are leaving Olympians, fans and aspiring young athletes wondering: why are women expected to bare their bodies while men cover up?

In April, the German women's gymnastics team ditched the traditional, high-cut leg-baring leotards for ankle-length unitards, protesting the 'sexualisation' of their bodies. This dissent was intended to highlight and prevent sexual abuse in the sport, following recent high-profile cases in the US and UK. They continued their protest at the Tokyo Olympics.

In a similar move, the Norwegian women's beach handball team were fined for defying the uniform rules at the European championships in July. In Tokyo, they too continued their protest by wearing fitted shorts. The team claimed bikini bottoms made them feel uncomfortable, made it difficult when managing their periods, and turned young athletes off their sport. For many, the last point is key to understanding the impact of sexist uniform policies.

Uniform rules in sport are designed for an idealised western femininity. These standards fail to understand that girls quit sport over body-baring uniforms, overlook different hair and skin types, ignore curvy and muscular body shapes and wilfully ignore the realities of periods. What these policies suggest is that women's bodies are expected to be perfectly thin, perfectly hairless, able-bodied and period-free.

British runner Jessica Ennis-Hill wrote a heartfelt essay about her fear of exposing herself and how 'skimpy kit' can traumatise young athletes. From body shaming to sexualisation, her experience exposes the unseen struggles of girls and women in sport and echoes research on girls in sport.

Overlooked and under-dressed

These campaigns reject sexist norms prevalent in sports and object to women's uniforms being designed for the 'male gaze', leading to women being judged for their aesthetic appeal alongside their athletic talent.

Undoubtedly, these women are taking a brave and laudable stance. Yet their voices carry an influence that women of colour and advocates for athletes in non-western countries are often denied. With much less fanfare and media attention, they have been lobbying for changes to kit for decades, often on behalf of Muslim athletes and/or people of colour.

In table tennis, a rule change for full-length sportswear and head coverings – as opposed to shorts and T-shirts which leave arms and legs bare – was successfully lobbied to increase participation by Muslim athletes. This victory went largely unnoticed in the west, despite the fact that table tennis is a mainstay of the Olympics. Campaigns led by Muslim athletes led to similar rule changes in basketball and judo, where women were finally allowed to wear head coverings and long-sleeved tops underneath, as their faith required.

In contrast, swimming has rejected proposals to adapt uniforms for Muslim and black athletes, including a ban on 'burkinis' and prohibiting use of the 'soul cap' swim hat designed for natural black hair.

Athletes with disabilities also face different standards, which was made clear recently when a British Paralympian was criticised by an official who called her outfit too 'revealing'. It was the standard runner's brief worn by most women.

Who makes the rules?

Modern sport was designed for and by white men. Globally, men are still making most of the rules, including those which police girls' and women's bodies. Regulations about uniforms vary by international federation, which is why the

Norwegian team faced fines but the Germans did not.

Although the International Olympic Committee (IOC) does not directly control uniform policies, it has advocated fairer rules in its 2018 Gender Equality Review to 'ensure competition uniforms reflect the technical requirements of the sport and do not have any unjustifiable differences'. This statement raises the question: what is the justifiable reason for requiring women to wear skimpy uniforms while men can cover up?

What does this mean for athletes and young girls with Olympic dreams? Beyond the general sexualisation of women athletes, there are six identifiable consequences that potentially harm girls and women in sport:

- Girls drop out of sport – adolescent girls feel too uncomfortable because of unflattering/exposing uniforms.

- Embarrassment – cameras can catch athletes accidentally exposing underwear, body hair and more. Mocking and body shaming on social media poses a real concern.

- Period panic – fear of leaking menstrual blood or exposing period products in skimpy or white clothing is common.

- Excluding athletes from non-western cultures – skin-exposing uniforms make it impossible for girls and women from Islamic and other religious communities to compete.

- Promoting racial prejudice – uniform standards often make assumptions about body types and hair built around white physical stereotypes.

- Battles over body hair – women and girls are pressured into waxing/shaving bikini lines, legs and any 'unfeminine' body hair or risk ridicule and body shaming on social media.

We need more women in leadership

These uniform policies put women under added pressure to conform to western feminine ideals when they should be concentrating on their athleticism. This constricting paradox leaves little room for agency among athletes to challenge traditional, negative conceptions about muscular femininity.

International federations need to adjust technical rules to allow for athletes to choose clothing that suits their performance, personal comfort and cultural preferences. These choices can motivate adolescent girls to remain in sport, support athletes of colour and encourage participation from more conservative cultures.

Recruiting more women from diverse backgrounds to leadership positions in sport is a key step. Broadcasters and marketers should take note – in the same way athletes feel uncomfortable, many women viewers do not enjoy watching sports with objectified bikini-clad players.

Generations of athletes and advocates have struggled to make these changes. More recently, the movement has gathered strength to band together across cultures and sports. The Olympics should be a place for inclusion, cultural exchange and equality. Let's start dressing the part.

5 August 2021

For Women's Euro 2022 to have a meaningful legacy, football must do more to tackle racism and sexism

An article from The Conversation.

THE CONVERSATION

By Jayne Caudwell, Associate Professor Social Sciences, Gender & Sexualities, Bournemouth University

Women have been playing football for a long time – and for a long time they have had to fight to be respected.

In 1969, the Daily Mirror used a photograph of a female footballer's shorts falling down while she jumped to head the ball. In the 1990s, players reported men walking across the pitch during women's football league games.

While Women's Euro 2022 has set new standards in terms of attendance and media coverage of the women's game, this generation of players continues to experience sexism.

Research carried out by broadcasters and media in Germany found that lewd remarks and other insults on social media were widespread during the 2022 Euros. Top-flight players in Germany reported experiencing sexism from journalists and coaches.

There is no official campaign against sexism in football from within the English Football Association. Ahead of the Euros, though, mobile network operator EE brought out an advertisement against online misogyny. The takeaway message was that 'sexist hate stops with men'.

Perhaps it's to be expected, given that brand activism is a well-known way to attract new consumers, that corporations are a step ahead of governing bodies in campaigns for equality. For instance, in the 1990s sports brand Nike sought out women consumers by focusing its campaigns on feminism and female empowerment.

Facing misogynoir

Misogyny encompasses more than just sexism. Girls and women are not a homogeneous group, and while some players will experience sexism, others will experience the intersections of sexism with racism.

The term 'misogynoir' is used to describe how racism and sexism combine and the specific way that Black women experience sexism. The body shaming and abuse directed at Serena Williams, one of the world's most successful tennis players, is one example.

In 2021, English player Rinsola Babajide received online abuse that denigrated her as a Black woman footballer. 'I just feel, as a Black woman in this game, I am conditioned to it,' Babajide told BBC News. 'It happens so regularly. It's more exhausting than anything. I've gone past the point of being disappointed or hurt by it.'

The spectacle of England's women winning Euro 2022 will drive change and progress. But from their first game on July 6 to the final, it was noticeable that every English starting lineup was made up of white players. There were only three Black players in the England squad of 23.

The whiteness of the current team may come as a surprise to some, because Black women have held visible roles in English women's football and continue to do so. Hope Powell was the first woman to coach England and continues her career managing Brighton & Hove Albion. Alex Scott and Eniola Aluko work in football commentary following successful playing careers.

Research shows that racism was and is embedded in both men's and women's football in England. The treatment of Aluko may have left a particular legacy: she experienced racism during her time as an England player, receiving degrading comments from management and coaching staff. After a long process which started in 2014, the FA made an apology in 2017.

Aluko felt that the FA had been dismissive when she first reported racism. Research by scholar Sara Ahmed shows how complaints made by women of colour are devalued, trivialised and often rejected – a process that can be racist in itself.

Sexist and racist abuse, as well as images of whiteness and the difficulties of calling out racism, may deter the next generations of players. If football is indeed a 'game for all', it must commit to diversity throughout the sport: from player development in schools through the structures of the game to the very top.

11 August 2022

Do sports stars need protection from media intrusion?

Are sports stars pampered youth not mature enough to handle wealth and fame? Or do journalists pick on them? The truth is in the middle.

By Paul Radford

Until Naomi Osaka withdrew from the French Open Tennis tournament last year after declining to attend the obligatory post-match press conference on the grounds of protecting her mental health, relatively little attention was paid to the potentially negative impact of media scrutiny on sports stars.

The Japanese player's stance, which cost her a $15,000 fine, has brought about a relaxation of the rigid rule, common to many sports, that every match should be followed by a press conference.

This year's tournament will offer alternative access in a so-called mixed zone where a player can talk to a handful of journalists in a more informal atmosphere.

Uneasy truce or solution to a growing problem of tensions between athletes and reporters? Are sports stars a set of pampered young people who have achieved wealth and fame before they are mature enough to handle it?

Or are journalists a bunch of would-be sports pros taking out their frustrations by picking on those who have succeeded where they have failed?

The truth, as ever, is probably somewhere in the middle.

Young sports stars are not seasoned politicians

As a Reuters journalist, I spent some 30 years covering elite sports all round the globe and have sat through hundreds of press conferences, some informative, some hilarious, but too many predictable, with repetitively dull questions from one side met by boring answers from the other.

I must admit I would have winced at the treatment Osaka received last year when she returned to the tennis circuit after taking a few months out to deal with her depression and mental health issues.

In her first press conference, she burst into tears when asked about how she balanced her dislike for such forums with the fact they gave her a media platform which benefited her outside interests. A reasonable question perhaps, but somewhat insensitive.

The kind of forensic questioning used to break down barriers put up by experienced politicians may not be suitable to employ on a young sports prodigy with little knowledge of life beyond training and competition.

More experienced athletes learn how to turn the tables on the journalists, of course, and I have been on the receiving end of an outburst or two.

'If you ask the same stupid questions, you'll get the same stupid answers.'

I once witnessed Australian Wimbledon champion Pat Cash lose horribly in straight sets to a relative nobody. In his frustration, he slammed his racket into the umpire's chair at the end of the match and received a warning.

It happened as journalists were leaving the press seats and none of us saw it, so I asked what I thought was an innocuous question at the subsequent press conference. 'What happened at the end of the match there, Pat?'

His face froze and he glared at me. He rose from his seat on the podium and came down to the front row where I was sitting, bent over me and put his face a few inches away from mine, staring straight into my eyes. Feeling threatened, I said nothing while returning his gaze.

After a few seconds, he straightened up and walked out of the press conference, saying: 'I'm not answering that.'

The legendary Martina Navratilova also took exception to an equally innocuous question I asked at a clay court tournament in Berlin.

I was interested in how she felt about her form on clay, her least favoured surface, ahead of the next Grand Slam tournament, the French Open. She gave me a non-committal answer, so I returned to the fray the following day having carefully rephrased my question.

She saw straight through it. 'Didn't you ask me this yesterday?' she boomed. 'Listen, if you ask the same stupid questions, you'll get the same stupid answers.' Game, set and match. No more questions from me for the rest of the tournament.

Answering to the media remains a vital task

Some superstars of their sports can be just as prickly outside of press conferences.

I once came across Olympic decathlon champion Daley Thompson at a publicity event. I politely introduced myself and asked whether I could have a few words. He offered me just two of his own, inviting me, in rather blunt terms, to go away.

Such incidents are easy to laugh off and retell as anecdotes of the life of the roving sports reporter. Not only are those of us who chronicle the world of sport not subjected to the same pressures to succeed as those we write about, we may, like it or not, contribute to those pressures.

A former Reuters colleague once described the mixed

Three questions to consider:

1. Should highly paid athletes be expected to face questions about their private life as well as their sporting career?

2. Do sports journalists owe a duty of care to young athletes suddenly thrust into the media spotlight?

3. Is it time to scrap formal press conferences and find ways of facilitating more informal contact between the media and athletes?

---

zones at the Olympic Games, where scores of journalists jostle to obtain quotes from athletes filing through on the other side of metal barriers, as 'a bear pit but with the animals on the outside looking in'.

Intimidating it may be, but answering to the media remains a vital task, both to promote individual sports and the image of the athlete, which ultimately determines his or her value to sponsors. Their eventual earnings in what is mostly a short career can depend upon it.

Plenty of sports personalities who thought they could shun the media and create their own brand through personal social media accounts have come a cropper. Their often-thoughtless posts, usually made as a joke, can reveal racist, homophobic or misogynistic tendencies that haunt them for years and may leave their reputations in tatters.

24 May 2022

Former global sports editor at Reuters, Paul Radford has covered 17 Olympic Games, seven World Cups and numerous world championships in more than 20 sports. He was sports editor for 12 years at the end of a career that included assignments in Germany and Paris. Formerly a consultant to the International Olympic Committee, he served on the IOC's press commission for 15 years and was editor-in-chief of the official Olympic News service at the 2014 Winter Olympics in Sochi, Russia.

Commonwealth Games 'ludicrous' drug testing row threatens expansion into esports

Esports leader says it's 'ludicrous' to expect them to adopt the same extensive anti-doping policy as conventional sport to become a full part of the Commonwealth Games.

By Aasma Day

In a fortnight's time thousands of excited spectators will be roaring on international sporting superstars at an elite event in Birmingham. Not the Commonwealth Games, but a parallel, linked competition taking place at the same time a short drive away across the city.

These sporting heroes won't be running, swimming or doing anything with balls. Their fingers are the only bit of their bodies they will need to move, because they will be playing computer games – or what are now known as electronic sports.

The decision to hold the Commonwealth Esports Championship in Birmingham while the main games take place in August is no coincidence, but part of an experiment that could see esports becoming a full part of the official Commonwealth Games by the end of the decade.

Two worlds are about to collide. And while the commitment to winning may be the same, they are very different in many other ways – including, *i* can reveal, policy on tackling drug cheats.

The Commonwealth Games will ensure competing athletes have been drug-tested and the event from 28 July to 8 August will be held under strict zero-tolerance rules

approved by the World Anti-Doping Agency (Wada) which bans a long list of substances from anabolic steroids to performance-enhancing amphetamines, masking agents and narcotics such as cannabis. But at the Commonwealth Esports Championships being on held on 6 and 7 August, there will be no drug-testing at all.

There is an esports list of banned substances in place – which includes drugs such as Adderall and Ritalin, commonly used to treat ADHD – which can aid concentration, focus and speed of reaction. But the commissioner responsible for the code has told *i* it will not be enforced in Birmingham because no prize money is at stake, only medals.

The Commonwealth Games Federation has indicated that will have to change if esports become a formal part of the games. But esports leaders are already signalling strong opposition. The man in charge of esports 'integrity' told *i* that applying the same anti-doping code would be 'a complete waste of time and money'.

It is likely to be a taste of sporting rows to come as the Commonwealth Games isn't the only global event looking at bringing esports into the fold. The International Olympic Committee has been making similar moves, with five associated esports events held in Tokyo ahead of last year's

games and insiders predicting there could be esports Olympic medal events at the 2028 Los Angeles games.

The attraction for the organisers of conventional sporting competitions can be summed up in one word – youth. Katie Sadleir, Commonwealth Games Federation chief executive, said the decision to sanction the esports championship in Birmingham came after discussions about ways the Games could capture the hearts and minds of the future.

Billion dollar electronic sport boom

Global esports revenues grew to $1.084 billion in 2021, a year-on-year rise of 14.5 per cent from $947.1 million in 2020 and up from $950.6 million in 2019, according to industry analyst Newzoo. That is predicted to grow to $1.38 billion by the end of 2022.

The figures dwarf those of some established conventional sports like rugby union. Governing body World Rugby reported revenues of $12.6 million in 2020. And even the $526 million from the men's Rugby World Cup year of 2019 was only half of what esports earned.

British stars like Jaden 'Wolfiez' Ashman have won fortunes from esports tournaments. The 18-year-old is a player of the Fortnite game and has earned prize money from 41 tournaments, believed to total $1,349,828.07. He has 796,000 followers on Twitch.

Competitors at inaugural Commonwealth Esports Championships in Birmingham in August will be playing Defense of the Ancients 2 – a multi-player fantasy 'battle arena' game; eFootball; and Rocket League – a video game described as 'soccer, but with rocket-powered cars'.

For those puzzled at how people can get so excited at watching people play video games, Andy Payne, chairman of the British Esports Federation, says it is akin to questioning why people enjoy watching live football or cricket.

'Watching esports is like being at any sporting event and there's a huge amount of passion, commitment and investment from fans,' he said. 'The atmosphere is intoxicating. Fans are really invested in the games, the players and the teams. It is almost primeval.'

He adds that esports' benefits include teamwork, promoting leadership, and helping people to make friends around the world – just like conventional sport then. But do electronic sports share the same problems? The existence of the Esports Integrity Commission (Esic) set up in 2016 to prevent 'cheating in esports, including... match manipulation and doping', suggests the risk, at least, is there.

And it is a risk others want to address. Ms Sadleir told *i* 'esports may well become part of the Commonwealth Games', suggesting it could happen by 2026. But her federation says that if it does, esports 'would need to be signed up to our anti-doping code aligned with all other sports at the Games'.

But the esports leaders disagree, partly because they think there is no need. 'People in sports get obsessed with doping, but it's not a thing in esports,' British Esports Federation chief executive Chester King said. 'That's not to

say it might not happen, but there are doping policies in place.'

Esic has an anti-doping code and a list of banned substances. But Ian Smith, commission head, says it has a different emphasis: 'With physical sports, doping is for strength and endurance. With esports, we are interested in stimulants that aid focus and speed of reaction.'

Mr Smith opposes the wider doping code the Commonwealth Federation would want esports to adopt, and says testing for online events would add to the expense.

'It would be a complete waste of time and money testing people for all these substances,' he said. 'If they ran an anti-doping programme at an esports event, they should use an esports-specific code like ours rather than a wider code that applies to people doing 100m sprints or boxing or swimming or weightlifting. It would be ludicrous.'

And this summer, Mr King is clear that 'there isn't any doping testing planned' for the Commonwealth Esports Championships. Because, he says, the event is about winning medals rather than money and also because 'doping is not an issue'.

'Is there drug testing at chess events or a poker event?' Mr King said. 'It's not something we have ever been concerned about.'

So while the twin events in Birmingham will demonstrate how two sporting worlds are coming together, they will also illustrate just how difficult a final union could be.

23 July 2022

Paralympic athletes call for major revisions to tackle doping

Concerns from international para-athletes and personnel raised over the integrity of para-sports.

By Professor Ian Boardley

Preserving the integrity of Paralympic sport is one of the key concerns of athletes taking part, and a project to understand ways to tackle para-sport doping heard from international athletes about their experiences and concerns.

The findings from the multi-agency Research-Embedded Strategic Plan for anti-doping Education: Clean sport alliance initiative for Tackling doping in Para-sport (RESPECT-P) project suggest a need for major policy revisions within Paralympic sport, including fixing issues with the classification system.

Findings from this Erasmus+ funded project were recently presented and discussed at the 3rd Clean Sport Insight Forum at the University of Birmingham, hosted by UK Anti- Doping (UKAD).

Through interviews with international para-athletes and athlete support personnel from six European countries, the project has identified significant threats to the integrity of ParaSport. During the forum, a panel of para-athletes including British powerlifter Ali Jawad, Dutch swimmer Liesette Bruinsma, and British wheelchair basketball and rugby player Gemma Lumsdaine discussed this issue, describing how the research findings resonated with their own experiences in para-sport.

Foremost amongst these threats are issues with the classification system, which determines the specific category that a particular para-athlete can compete within. Although this system aims to ensure only athletes with similar levels of impairment compete against each other, the RESPECT-P project has discovered significant potential for the system to be abused. Specifically, athletes can intentionally misrepresent the degree or nature of their impairment to allow them to compete against athletes with greater levels of impairment and gain a performance advantage.

Other threats to the integrity of para-sport identified through the project include misuse of the Therapeutic Use Exemption system to allow sanctioned use of prohibited substances, manipulation of equipment to gain an unfair advantage, and intentional induction of autonomic dysreflexia with the aim of enhancing performance (aka 'boosting') through stimulation of the autonomic nervous system (e.g., increased heart rate and blood pressure).

> *'To protect Clean Para-Sport, we need to find suitable solutions for all relevant integrity issues, which include – but are not restricted to – doping.'*
>
> - Dr Ian Boardley, Reader in Sport and Exercise Psychology

Implementing effective policies

During the forum, an expert panel including Professor Andrea Petroczi, Dr Tom Nightingale, and Ali Jawad discussed the significant challenges to implementing effective policies to address these threats to the integrity of para-sport. Although there are significant challenges, there was general consensus that we shouldn't shy away from difficult problems, and that researchers, practitioners, policy makers, and athletes should work together to find suitable solutions.

Another issue that was discussed during the forum was the lack of evidence relating to the prevalence of these integrity issues. It is likely that some sports and/or impairments are more susceptible to each specific issue, but the lack of robust prevalence data makes it difficult to understand which one poses the greatest threat and therefore where to focus research attention and funding. Thus, speakers throughout the day called for more research into prevalence of these integrity issues within ParaSport and more funding to look at these complex issues in detail.

A further discussion point throughout the day was how athletes define the term 'Clean Sport'. Although this term is often connected with anti-doping and drug-free sport, it is evident both from the project findings and discussions during the forum that athletes view Clean Sport as more than doping-free sport. Specifically, they view it as being synonymous with high levels of integrity across the board, and therefore more representative of cheating-free sport. Thus, to protect Clean Para-Sport, we need to find suitable solutions for all relevant integrity issues, which include – but are not restricted to – doping.

The 4th Clean Sport Insight Forum will take place on 22nd November 2022 in Muenster, Germany and will discuss system perspectives and the future directions.

21 July 2022

Lack of action on corruption, abuse and financial profiteering in sport could lead to a public inquiry

By David Lavallee

Having been appointed to the role of Professor of Duty of Care in Sport at Abertay University in Scotland four years ago, I have studied how major sport organisations across the globe respond to investigations associated with a range of mistreatment issues, including abuse, bullying and manipulation ever since in order to better understand the importance of sport in our lives. At the start, I believed the sports organisations concerned would not step back from issues within their own control, but step forward and see such investigations as opportunities to learn from its own experience. I believed the scale and scope of the response by sports organisations would match the size of the problem and that people who made mistakes would be held responsible, instead of being allowed to blame the system.

I believed people who participate in sport would be protected and no longer be seen as commodities and that the number of negative cases related to fraud, bullying and misconduct would decrease. I believed sport would progress beyond the obsession of winning, and would capitalise on its unique ability for all people to cooperate and support each other as part of a team.

I believed victims of bullying, harassment and discrimination would be comprehensively supported at the point of need and that the people who engage in such unacceptable behaviour, along with their protectors and enablers, could be rehabilitated as part of an effective duty of care system. I believed sport systems would come together in a coordinated way to share successes and best practice and, ultimately, become more sustainable.

Finally, I believed sport would be seen as a leading sector across society for refusing to become conditioned to accepting the mistreatment of people and having an unacceptable tolerance of such behaviour. Having now researched 24 sport investigations across five countries over this period, my beliefs have changed.

I now believe the sport system is irradicably trapped in a bad way. There are some very capable leaders and managers who have good intentions and have genuinely tried to take action within their own sport during this period of extraordinary crisis.

It is also hard to imagine how player associations could do any more to protect human rights, ensure the voice of their participants is heard and work to make their sport safe. But the structures in place and ways of operating within the organisations controlling sport are so deeply entrenched that I believe any system-wide reform for the better is now impossible. There was a genuine opportunity for this following the Duty of Care in Sport Review by Baroness Tanni Grey-Thompson four years ago, but unfortunately I think that time has now passed.

I now believe that many of the conditions are in place for a statutory public inquiry to be established specifically related to sport. Across society, there appears to be increasing expectation that public inquiries are the only tool that can address institutional failures and uncover the truth. There are also now clear commonalities and patterns that show the issues blighting sport are of a similar scale and grave nature to events that led to inquiries of major public concern, including child abuse, the global banking collapse and others.

For example following accusations, the approach across the organisations concerned is to take the middle ground and indicate that action will be taken. Both distant promises and quick-fix solutions are proclaimed over time to create an impression of progress. The language is changed, always using the furtive term, culture. New strategies are developed without a clear set of choices, and also for longer and longer periods of time. The institutions involved then seep as far back as possible over several years to their previous position, sometimes exceeding it, while trustworthiness gradually erodes away through this never-ending cycle.

To be clear, I am not calling for a public inquiry to be set up. Just imagine what 365+ days of public hearings, hundreds of witnesses from State and non-State institutions legally compelled to give evidence, hundreds of thousands of disclosed documents, texts and email communications released, series after series of reports and a colossal budget would do to the sport system. I would never wish to see this come about, as I believe the fallout would inadvertently erode trust beyond a tipping point, but I do now worry sport could be one major case away to this action being taken.

As a result of my changed beliefs, I have fundamentally shifted my approach to research and initiated a new field of knowledge, named Sports Forensic. This involves working in collaboration with organisations such as INTERPOL and KPMG to support raising awareness and to help sports respond to issues associated with fraud, bullying and misconduct.

It's been a turbulent period for all sports, not least due to the challenges presented by the pandemic. But soon, the eyes of the world will be firmly back on sport as the Olympic and Paralympic flame makes its way to Tokyo. The future of sport is at a crossroads. An obsession with winning, monetisation, and a total lack of regard for people who are mistreated in pursuit of these goals lies down one path; and participant welfare and all the potential health, community and economic impacts lies down the other.

I believe sport organisations are left with a binary option: continue to drift into the abyss or make every sacrifice to prevent the mistreatment of every single one of their participants from ever happening. I hope they choose the latter.

9 July 2021

Greed no match for fans' fury as football Super League fails

Owners of rich European football clubs thought a Super League would line their pockets. They failed to consider outraged fans — the ultimate bosses.

By John Mehaffey

Unprecedented English fan power in the country that invented football makes it unlikely any European soccer club owners will ever attempt to launch an exclusive elite competition after a proposed European Super League collapsed just three days after it was announced.

Under the plan, Manchester United, Manchester City, Liverpool, Arsenal, Chelsea and Tottenham were to join Spain's Real Madrid, Atletico Madrid and Barcelona plus Italian clubs AC Milan, Inter Milan and Juventus in an annual competition eventually comprising 20 teams.

The announcement last month was immediately denounced by the bodies that govern European and world football.

But what really forced the owners to drop their plan were the spontaneous demonstrations in England outside stadiums and at training grounds by fans outraged at the proposal to have 15 permanent members of the Super League with no promotion or relegation.

Each season, the three bottom teams in the English Premier League are relegated and three from the second division are promoted.

Thus, the proposed Super League would have resembled the four major U.S. sports of American football, basketball, baseball and ice hockey, which don't see new, up-and-coming teams added to their list each year or those with the worst records dropped.

European football fans love the drama of relegation and promotion

The drama generated by the structure of the English Premier League has helped to make it the world's most popular soccer tournament. It is broadcast in 189 territories around the world to an estimated annual audience of over one billion viewers, with 65% of them in Asia and Oceania.

Cinderella tales of unheralded teams rising through the professional ranks to challenge established powers are part and parcel of the sport's history in Europe. Millions of fans take a keen interest not only in who emerges at the top of the table but also in which teams will suffer the ignominy of relegation and which will earn heady promotion.

Take Leicester City, a team based in the east Midlands of England. In the 2013-14 season, they won the third division, then the second division to reach the top Premier League. Two seasons later, they won the Premier League in one of the biggest shocks in the history of English soccer, which led to record payouts by bookmakers.

This month, Leicester upset Chelsea — which would have been one of the Super League teams — in the Football Association final, the knockout competition that is the oldest soccer tournament in the world and which features all the professional league clubs plus hundreds of non-League teams.

So many fans saw the Super League as an elitist group of rich teams that would sideline most clubs. What is more, the owners backing the Super League were seen as motivated more by their appetite for money than any love of the game.

'At the heart of the European football, in fact football everywhere but in the U.S., is the concept of promotion and relegation,' said former Reuters Soccer Editor and soccer historian Mike Collett.

'They utterly failed to display any understanding of the social roots of football that have existed in effect since 1888, when the Football League was founded and then the second division with promotion and relegation was introduced. They were happy to stamp on 130 years of history. For what? A concept no one wanted.'

Big U.S. bank was bankrolling the proposed Super League

Money is the driving force behind most professional sports, and so it was with the aborted Super League.

U.S. investment bank JPMorgan Chase had agreed to underwrite an initial 3.5 billion euro investment to help the 12 football clubs set up the proposed Super League, according to Bloomberg News.

The Super League would have effectively replaced the Champions League, Europe's current club championship, which generates around three billion euros of revenue each year. That may sound like a lot of money, but it pales in comparison with the estimated $12 billion of income that, according to magazine Sports Illustrated, the U.S. National Football League produced last year.

Three questions to consider:

1. Why were many English football fans upset over the European Super League proposal?

2. What was JPMorgan Chase's role in the proposal?

3. Do you think that money plays too big a role in professional sports?

Organizers of the Super League were hoping its competition would bring in more revenue — including billions through televison rights — than the Champions League, which brings together the leading teams from Europe's domestic leagues in an annual tournament watched by millions.

Teams in the Super League were also hoping that they would continue to pocket income from their domestic leagues.

Some critics of the Super League said the U.S. investment bank had failed to appreciate fans' attachment to the longstanding system in European leagues that offers hope, however faint, to clubs from small cities and towns that someday they can play in the big league.

Owners of those clubs may not boast the hefty bankrolls of their exalted peers in the big urban centres, padded by massive TV payouts, that allows them to attract the world's best and most expensive players. But fans around the world love an underdog, and there seemed little room for longshots in the proposed Super League.

'Another attempt is unrealistic'

Still, JPMorgan, which has operations around the world, is no newcomer to European football.

According to Bloomberg, the investment bank's links to big deals in the sport go back almost two decades. It has advised Manchester United as well as the buyers of both Fiorentina and Roma in Italy, and helped Inter Milan, Roma and Real Madrid raise money, the news service said.

News reports have noted that the owners of three of the English teams that signed up for the Super League — Manchester United, Arsenal and Liverpool — are Americans who backed another aborted super league project floated in 2009 that would have been bankrolled by another U.S. investment bank, Morgan Stanley.

Whether it was due to sheer greed, misjudgment or a combination of the two on the part of the club owners, the plan quickly collapsed amid outrage vented by fans, politicians and football's governing bodies.

'The incredible thing to come out of this was the unity of the fans,' Collett said. 'It did not matter if you supported Liverpool, Tottenham, Arsenal, Chelsea or whoever, the fans were united in a way I had never seen before in 50-plus years' involvement in football.'

Collett continued: 'The overwhelming opposition to the idea makes it unrealistic to believe any owner in the future will attempt this again. I believe the game is safe from such an unpopular move. This was a total miscalculation by the owners. They totally and utterly failed to understand the fury of the fans.'

20 May 2021

John Mehaffey has worked for four decades as a journalist in New Zealand, Australia and Britain, including 33 on the Reuters Sports Desk covering seven summer Olympics plus World Cups and world championships in athletics, soccer, cricket, rugby, amateur boxing and gymnastics. He wrote extensively on sports news including drugs in sport, the readmission of South Africa to international sport and corruption in cricket. He was appointed Chief Sports Reporter in 2001.

Key Facts

- England's women's football team won the Euros in 2022. Attendance at the match was 87,192, the biggest crowd for a Euros football match for either men's or women's football. (page 1)

- Break dancing will be included in the Paris 2024 Olympics. (page 3)

- The Olympic Games began in Greece in 776 BCE. (page 4)

- Early sporting heroes included runner Leonidas of Rhodes, who won 12 gold medals, a feat unrivalled until American swimmer Michael Phelps secured his 13th Olympic title in 2016. (page 4)

- The modern Olympics were the brainchild of French aristocrat Pierre de Coubertin. Through his efforts, the modern Olympics were launched in Athens in 1896. Barring two world wars and now a global pandemic, they have been held every four years since. (pages 4-5)

- Activity levels dropped during the pandemic but are now showing signs of partial recovery. (page 11)

- Of those activities showing growth before the pandemic, only walking for leisure (+2.4m up to 24m) has continued to see numbers rise. (page 12)

- More than 185 rugby players have launched legal proceedings against World Rugby, the Rugby Football Union and Welsh Rugby Union. (page 14)

- New research by Ipsos in the UK shows more than one in four football and rugby union fans do not think enough is being done to combat concussions in professional football and rugby union. (page 16)

- Before the pandemic, netball was increasing in popularity and participation levels were at an all-time high. (page 19)

- The ASICS Uplifting Minds study found that stopping exercise for a week has the same effect on your mental wellbeing as seven nights of broken sleep, with significant falls in areas including confidence levels, energy and ability to cope with stress. (page 19)

- The study also found that just 15 minutes and nine seconds (of exercise) is enough to significantly improve our state of mind. (page 19)

- The sporting statues project database has recorded statues around the world of more than 750 different football players and managers – but only seven are from the women's game – and all were erected in the past decade. (page 21)

- The US has more than 300 baseball statues, yet only two are of female players. Across the UK, of the 220 sportspeople who have been honoured by statues, only three are women. (page 21)

- Of the UK's 220 subject-specific sports statues, almost half depict footballers (106), with rugby players (15) or cricketers (10) also featuring regularly. (page 21)

- A study published last year in the British Journal of Sports Medicine found that trans women who underwent hormone therapy for one year continued to maintain an athletic advantage, despite a 15-31 per cent decline in physical performance. (page 23)

- The Welsh national football association has pledged to introduce equal pay for their men's and women's teams by 2026. (page 26)

- In 2019 the US women's national football team took the US Soccer Federation to court in pursuit of better pay and working conditions. At the time, an economic expert noted the women's team could be owed US$66 million (£48.2 million). (page 26)

- In UK schools as a whole, only 63 per cent offer girls the chance to play football as much as the boys in P.E. The numbers are even worse in secondary school; it's 72 per cent in primary school, but 44 per cent from Year 7 onwards. (page 28)

- There is an esports list of banned substances in place – which includes drugs such as Adderall and Ritalin, commonly used to treat ADHD – which can aid concentration, focus and speed of reaction. (page 34)

- The English Premier League is the world's most popular soccer tournament. It is broadcast in 189 territories around the world to an estimated annual audience of over one billion viewers, with 65% of them in Asia and Oceania. (page 38)

Anabolic steroids

Anabolic steroid is a blanket term for drugs which mimic the effects of male reproductive hormones, i.e. by boosting muscle growth and protein synthesis. Side effects such as aggression, liver damage and high blood pressure can be very harmful. Some athletes take them legally in order to improve their performance; people who use performance-enhancing drugs in excess sometimes don't even view themselves as 'drug addicts', but rather that they are healthy people who are taking pride in their appearance.

Athlete

A highly trained professional or amateur sportsman/woman.

Commonwealth Games

The Commonwealth Games, sometimes known as the Friendly Games, are a quadrennial international multi-sport event among athletes from the Commonwealth of Nations. The event was first held in 1930, and, with the exception of 1942 and 1946, have successively run every four years since.

Doping

The use of performance-enhancing drugs by athletes during sporting competitions. Most of these drugs are illegal and athletes are require by law to take a drugs test before taking part in competitive events. If it is found that they have taken drugs they will automatically be disqualified from the event and may also be banned from taking part in any future competitions for a period of time.

Elite athlete

A person who is currently or has previously competed as a varsity player (individual or team), a professional player or a national or international level player.

eSports

Esports or 'electronic sports' is a term used to describe organized competitive video-gaming, especially among professional gamers.

Gender pay gap

At EU level, the gender pay gap is defined as the relative difference in the average gross hourly earnings of women and men within the economy as a whole.

Inclusive sport

Sport which is inclusive and does not discriminate on the grounds of gender, ethnicity, sexual orientation or disability. Sport is usually segregated where athletes have a physical difference which makes equal competition difficult – men and women do not generally compete against each other, for example, nor disabled or able-bodied athletes. This is called classification, However there is no ban on any athlete competing in a separate competition. This why the term 'sport equity' is sometimes used rather than equality. Athletes should be protected from discrimination and unfair treatment, such as racist and homophobic chanting at football matches.

Olympic Games

Every four years the Olympic Games are held in a different city around the world. The next summer Olympic Games which will take place in 2024 are to be held in Paris.

Paralympic Games

The Paralympic Games are a series of sporting competitions open to athletes with physical disabilities. They are held immediately following the Olympic Games. Athletes with disabilities including amputations, paralysis and blindness take part in a wide range of competitive sports.

Physical activity

Physical activity includes all forms of activity, such as walking or cycling, active play, work-related activity, active recreation such as working out in a gym, dancing, gardening or competitive sport like football. Regular physical activity can reduce the risk of many chronic health conditions including coronary heart disease, type 2 diabetes, cancer and obesity. Regular physical activity also has positive benefits for mental health as it can reduce anxiety and enhance moods and self-esteem, which reduces the risk of depression.

Rugby scrum

A scrum (short for scrummage) is a method of restarting play in rugby that involves players packing closely together with their heads down attempting to gain possession of the ball. Depending on whether it is in rugby union or rugby league the scrum is utilised after either an accidental infringement or when the ball has gone out of play.

Winter Olympic Games

The Winter Olympic Games is a multi-sport international competition held once every four years for sports practised on snow and ice. The first Winter Olympics were held in Chamonix, France in 1924.

Activities

Brainstorming

◆ As a class, brainstorm a list of the most prominent sport-related news stories that have caught your attention over the last year or so.

◆ What is doping?

◆ What is eSport?

◆ What are the Commonwealth Games?

◆ Where are the next Olympic Games going to be held?

Research

◆ Do some research into a new sport or fitness activity that you have always wanted to try. Find out as much as you can about it, including how popular it is and if it is available near where you live. Create a factsheet about the sport/activity.

◆ In pairs do some research into the different types of sport in which paralympians can participate. Do the sports available vary in different countries?

◆ In small groups do some research into ticket prices charged by various football clubs in the UK. Produce a graph to show your findings with the rest of the class. Do you think the ticket prices are justified?

◆ Do some online research into the problem of doping in sport. How many news stories can you find about doping scandals over the last couple of years? Choose the one you find most interesting and share a summary of it with your class.

◆ Conduct a questionnaire amongst your family and/or friends to find out how much exercise they do each week. Produce a graph to demonstrate your findings in the following categories:

· Type of activity

· Frequency per week

· Age group

· Gender

Design

◆ Choose one of the articles from this book and create an illustration that highlights its key message.

◆ Design a poster to be displayed at your school/college aimed at encouraging more students to participate in sports.

◆ In small groups, choose a sport and design a new piece of protective kit or equipment for participants to use. It could be to protect their heads, or perhaps another part of their body. Come up with a suitable name for it and present it to the rest of the class.

◆ In pairs, create a social media campaign warning against the dangers of misusing performance- enhancing drugs such as anabolic steroids. Highlight the physical and psychological side effects that can affect both men & women who use them regularly.

Oral

◆ Read the article *Paris 2024: The new sports at the next Olympics and the ones that won't be there* on page 3. What are your thoughts about the sports that are being included in the Olympic timetable for the very first time? Are there any other sports you think should be included? Are there any sports you think should be dropped? As a class, discuss your suggestions and the reasoning behind them.

◆ In pairs, talk about the gender pay gap in professional sport. What sport has the biggest wage gap? What are the main reasons for the pay difference? What do you think should be done to achieve equal pay for women in sport?

◆ Split the class into two to debate the question: 'Should all drugs be banned in sport?'

Reading/writing

◆ Select an article from this book and write a short summary highlighting its key points.

◆ Write a blogpost about a sport or physical exercise that you enjoy. Describe how it makes you feel and the benefits it brings to your life.

◆ Imagine you are an agony Aunt/Uncle. A 13-year-old gymnast has written to you saying a member of the coaching team is making inappropriate remarks to them and making them feel uncomfortable. They are worried if they speak out they might get dropped from the squad. Write a suitable response giving them advice on where they might find help and support.

Acknowledgements

The publisher is grateful for permission to reproduce the material in this book. While every care has been taken to trace and acknowledge copyright, the publisher tenders its apology for any accidental infringement or where copyright has proved untraceable. The publisher would be pleased to come to a suitable arrangement in any such case with the rightful owner.

The material reproduced in **issues** books is provided as an educational resource only. The views, opinions and information contained within reprinted material in **issues** books do not necessarily represent those of Independence Educational Publishers and its employees.

Images

Cover image courtesy of iStock. All other images courtesy Freepik, Pixabay & Unsplash except pages 17, 19 & 20: iStock.

Additional acknowledgements

With thanks to the Independence team: Shelley Baldry, Tracy Biram, Klaudia Sommer and Jackie Staines.

Danielle Lobban

Cambridge, September 2022